Message's From Heaven Above

James Andrew Feather 1st

Bloomington, IN

authorHOUSE™

Milton Keynes, UK

AuthorHouse™
1663 Liberty Drive, Suite 200
Bloomington, IN 47403
www.authorhouse.com
Phone: 1-800-839-8640

AuthorHouse™ UK Ltd.
500 Avebury Boulevard
Central Milton Keynes, MK9 2BE
www.authorhouse.co.uk
Phone: 08001974150

First published by AuthorHouse 4/6/2006

ISBN: 1-4259-1906-5 (sc)

Printed in the United States of America
Bloomington, Indiana

This book is printed on acid-free paper.

A SPECIAL THANKS

I want to thank these special individuals for their help in making the publication of this book possible. Their love is truly appreciated by me, and I pray Gods blessings on them and their families. I want to recognize these loved ones in these first printed books, by sharing their names with you. I want to especially thank Michael Sanders for the design of the front cover.

I pray that this book glorifies our Lord Jesus in a mighty way! After all, it is **his** book!

1: Michael Sanders
2: Kim and Tom Gearrin
3: James Chisholm
4: Bertha Odom
5: Donna and Garry Curtis
6: Andrew Feather
7: Evelyn and Paul Toms
8: Margaret Barber
9: John Foster
10: Veldres and Jewel Baxter
11: Deddie and Stoney Kiser
12: Molly and Russell Zablan Jr.
13: Faith Wilson
14: Sandra and David Strickler
15: Athaleen and Frank Garner
16: Tiffany and Jeremy Pullen
17: Amy and Matt Bolton
18: Jean and Bill Staneck
19: Linda Martin
20: Sherakery Grace
21: Francis Martin
22: Kelly and Randle Willis
23: Tess Kaye

INTRODUCTION

This book came about when I was asked by my church to be the Sunday School Director. Part of my duty was to give a devotional before Sunday school, in our General Assembly.

I could have used someone else's devotional; but I really wanted God to be the one to reveal his word to us. So I prayed, read my Bible, and waited every time for God's Message. I thank and praise God, that he always gave me a message for our church!

The messages in this book are just some of God's messages, and I pray that God will share his meaning to you as you read them. Enjoy your fellowship with him and give him the glory! He sent our precious Savior Jesus, to do so much more than save us from our sins. He was raised from the dead to give us eternal life! He also lived on this earth to show us how we should live our lives.

When he went home to be with our heavenly Father, he left the Holy Ghost here; to teach us, convict us, and empower us as Christians. Jesus has done most of the work for us. I say most, because it is our responsibility to accept him as our sacrifice for sins that we committed! He will not force him self upon us!

Enjoy his grace and love, and follow him everyday. He really does love you!

I thank God for allowing me to be an ink pen for him; but all the glory is his!

James Andrew Feather 1st

Contents

A GREAT LIGHT ROUND ABOUT ME!

(Acts 22:4-9)

4) And I persecuted this way unto the death, binding and delivering into the prisons both men and women.

5) As also the high priest doth bear me witness, and all the estate of the elders: from whom also I received letters from the brethren, and went to Damascus, to bring them which were there bound unto Jerusalem, for to be punished.

6) And it came to pass, that, as I made my journey, and was come nigh unto Damascus about noon, suddenly there shone from Heaven a great light round about me.

7) And I fell unto the ground, and heard a voice saying unto me, Saul, Saul, why persecutest thou me?

8) And I answered, who art thou, Lord? And he said unto me, I am Jesus of Nazareth, whom thou persecutest.

9) And they that were with me saw indeed the light, and were afraid: but they heard not the voice of him that spake to me.

Here is a normal bright sunny day. You are walking along going to another city, and all of a sudden a bright light falls upon you! A light that is so bright that it shines far brighter than the sun. Can you even imagine a light this bright?

This is the beginning of Paul's testimony unto the Jews. And as you read all of his testimony, you find out that he worked for the high priests to capture and persecute those who were speaking about this Jesus of Nazareth.

Why do you think Jesus would choose such a man to be a prophet? Paul tortured and killed some of Jesus' saints! Because of the testimony that Paul had, I believe that Paul was a man with unending dedication in what he believed in. I believe Paul was full of passion. I believe that Jesus heard the prayers of all the Saints that were tortured and put to death by Paul. I believe that God would receive the most glory by Paul changing his ways than any other man at that time. I also feel that Jesus showed all of us that he loves us so much, that he is willing to even forgive us for persecuting him!

Now his ex-enemy Paul is a brother in arms, fighting the cause of truth and love! Have you seen a bright light go off in your heart? Has Jesus called out your name? Come to know this amazing savior that is known as Jesus of Nazareth! He is Gods only son! And he knows you, and still loves you very much!

Repent of your sins and serve the one and only true Savior, Jesus!

A LOVING FATHER

One day a loving father called his son to come to him. When the son arrived he immediately asked what was wrong. The son knew there was a problem, by the tears in his father's eyes. The father replied that all his other children were in serious danger. They had gotten off the road he told them to take, and now they were very lost. The road that they were taking was filled with very bad people; and these people were going to hurt and torture them if they get their hands on them. The son immediately replies;" Let me go to them", "Let me save them." The father then told his loving son that to save his brothers and sisters lives that he himself would have to give up his own life. The son said that "I do not care"," I love them." "I know you do son." "That is why I am going to send you to be their savior."

The father said "Okay son, go and show them the way home." "Bring them here yourself, and remember that I will be with you every step of the way." With that being said; ***Jesus*** left heaven and came to earth to save us from our sins and the penalty for them, which is death...

(John 3:16)

For God so loved the world, that he gave his only begotten Son, that whosoever believeth in him should not perish, but have everlasting life.

A PROPHET IS NOT WITHOUT HONOR!

(Mark 6:3)

When **Jesus** *returned back into his own country; and preached in a synagogue on a Sabbath day; even though those that heard him preach were astonished, they doubted him because they knew him his entire life. They said, Is not this the carpenter, the son of Mary, the brother of James, and Jo'ses, and of Juda, and Simon? And are not his sisters here with us? And they were offended at him.*

(Mark 6:5)

And he could there do no mighty work, save that he laid his hands upon a few sick folk, and healed them.

So because of their doubt, they took away a lot of miracles from **Jesus** that he was planning to do there. A lot of people were not healed, or devils were not cast out. But more importantly, the word of **God** was not believed.

(Mark 6:4)

But **Jesus** *said unto them, a prophet is not without honour, but in his own country, and among his own kin, and in his own house.*

Jesus understood that he was not being taken seriously there. And his preaching was not going to help them, because of their unbelief and doubt.

So do not get frustrated if there is doubt and no honor in your testimony in your home, or in your family. Continue to serve **Jesus** everywhere it is welcomed. **Jesus** will send other children to minister to your family. After all, we really want the honor to go to **Jesus** anyway!

A WOMAN DISCIPLE?

(Acts 9:36 thru 41)

36) Now there was at Jop`pa a certain disciple named Tab`-i-tha, which by interpretation is called Dor`-cas: this woman was full of good works and alms deeds which she did.

37) And it came to pass in those days, that she was sick, and died: whom when they had washed, they laid her in an upper chamber.

38) And forasmuch as Lyd`-da was nigh to Jop`-pa, and the disciples had heard that Peter was there, they sent unto him two men, desiring him that he would not delay to come to them.

39) Then Peter arose and went with them. When he was come, they brought him into the upper chamber: and all the widows stood by him weeping and shewing the coats and garments which Dor`-cas made, while she was with them.

40) But Peter put them all forth, and kneeled down, and prayed; and turning him to the body said Tab`-i-tha, arise. And she opened her eyes: and when she saw Peter, she sat up.

41) And he gave her his hand, and lifted her up, and when he had called the saints and widows, presented her alive.

Now there are many things to take notice of in this awesome story. First point is that there was, and still are women disciples. This woman was a worker for God, doing all kind of good for the widows and others in her area. Teaching the word of God as she helped them; thus the reason she was called a disciple, and not just a kind woman.

God was poised to perform another miracle in the woman's town. He set it up that Peter was in the area at the time of Tabitha's death. Why do you think that he needed Peter to be there, and not some other disciple? Could it be that no one else's heart was right?

Or maybe he was still making Peter's testimony strong, so that the people would believe him when he preached the word of God.

It was, and still is important for the people to actually see great things happen before their own eyes; because there are still a lot of them not willing to believe in something they cannot see!

The point is; is that miracles are real! God still performs them through saints who have given themselves unto the Lord. Miracles still happen today! You only have to ask God for them; and then believe he will answer your prayer.

Notice also how Peter got on his knees to pray. In asking an almighty God for something you desire, make sure that you show the proper respect to God, and make sure that it is he that receives the glory!

ABIDE IN MY LOVE!

(John 15: 10 thru 13)

10) If ye keep my commandments, ye shall abide in my love; even as I have kept my Father's commandments, and abide in his love.

11) These things have I spoken unto you, that my joy might remain in you, and that your joy might be full.

12) This is my commandment, that ye love one another, as I have loved you.

13) Greater love hath no man than this that a man lay down his life for his friends.

How much easier can Jesus make it for us all? He tells us how we should love everyone else as he has loved us, and if you accept him as your savior, then he gives us the ability to have un-ending love through the power of the Holy Spirit!

If you are a Christian, then you understand this statement, and know that it is true. If you do not understand this never ending love, then call out to Jesus; and ask him how you may have joy and love in your life.

Do you abide in him? Or does your love have limitations?

AM I ONLY DREAMING?

(Acts 12:4 thru 11)

4) And when he had apprehended him, he put him in prison, and delivered him to four quaternions of soldiers to keep him; intending after Easter to bring him forth to the people.

So King Herod has captured Peter and thrown him in prison. He intends to let the people cast judgment on him after Easter.

5) Peter therefore was kept in prison: but prayer was made without ceasing of the church unto God for him.

The church heard what Herod had done to Peter and prayed to God for Peter's safety. They prayed without ceasing!

6) And when Herod would have brought him forth, the same night Peter was sleeping between two soldiers, bound with two chains: and the keepers before the door kept the prison.

Notice how many guards were assigned to watch over Peter. He slept between two guards while also being chained; and two more guards were in front of the door of his cell. The only crime Peter had done was preaching God's word and doing good deeds.

7) And, behold, the angel of the Lord came upon him, and a light shined in the prison: and he smote Peter on the side, and raised him up, saying, Arise up quickly. And his chains fell off from his hands.

The angel of the Lord had entered the cell with Peter and the guards, and the Bible says that the entire prison was lit up. The angel poked Peter in the side and woke him up. When Peter rose up the chains fell off his hands.

8) And the angel said unto him, Gird thyself, and bind on thy sandals. And so he did. And he saith unto him, cast thy garment about thee, and follow me.

9) And he went out, and followed him: and wist not that it was true which was done by the angel; but thought he saw a vision.

The angel told Peter to put on his clothes and follow him. While they were going out of the cell Peter wondered if he was only dreaming. Even though he was seeing and feeling it all, he still had doubt.

10) When they were past the first and second ward, they came unto the Iron Gate that leadeth unto the city; which opened to them of his own accord: and they went out, and passed on through one street; and forthwith the angel departed from him.

11) And when Peter was come to himself, he said; now I know of a surety, that the Lord hath sent his angel, and hath delivered me out of the hand of Herod, and from all the expectation of the people of the Jews.

It was not until Peter was walking on the street of the city that he realized what was happening was real. That God had really sent an angel to give him his freedom. So next time God sends you an angel to free you from persecution; believe it!

ARE YOU SAVED OR JUST BAPTIZED?

(Acts 8:6 thru 13)

6) And the people with one accord gave heed unto those things which Philip spake, hearing and seeing the miracles which he did.

7) For unclean spirits, crying with loud voice came out of many that were possessed with them; and many taken with palsies, and that were lame, were healed.

8) And there was great joy in that city.

9) But there was a certain man, called Simon, which before time in the same city used sorcery, and bewitched the people of Sa-ma`-ri-a, giving out that himself was some great one:

10) To whom they all gave heed, from the least to the greatest, saying, this man is the great power of God.

11) And to him they had regard, because that of long time he had bewitched them with sorceries.

12) But when they believed Philip preaching the things concerning the kingdom of God, and the name of Jesus Christ, they were baptized, both men and women.

13) Then Simon himself believed also: and when he was baptized, he continued with Philip, and wondered, beholding the miracles and signs which were done.

Now you might be excited that there were so many people who believed in the word of God and were baptized. But were they all born again? Did they become true children of our almighty God, or just believers?

(Acts 8:14 thru 17)

14) Now when the apostles, which were at Jerusalem, heard that Sa-ma`-ri-a received the word of God, they sent unto them Peter and John:

15) Who, when they were come down, prayed for them, that they might receive the Holy Ghost?

16) (For as yet he was fallen upon none of them: only they were baptized in the name of the Lord Jesus.)

17) Then laid they their hands on them, and they received the Holy Ghost.

WOW! I wonder how many of my family and friends are only baptized with water, and not with the Holy Spirit! How can I be sure of which are truly born again?

This is not my job to do! Jesus and he alone will judge us all! But out of my love for them all, I can, and will pray for them that they are blessed with the Holy Spirit in their hearts.

(Acts 8:18 thru 22)

18) And when Simon saw that through laying on of the apostles' hands the Holy Ghost was given, he offered them money,

19) Saying, give me also the power that on whomsoever I lay hands; he may receive the Holy Ghost.

20) But Peter said unto him, Thy money perish with thee, because thou hast thought that the gift of God may be purchased with money.

21) Thou hast neither part nor lot in this matter: for thy heart is not right in the sight of God.

22) Repent therefore of this thy wickedness, and pray God, if perhaps the thought of thine heart be forgiven thee.

Is it time to look into your own heart? What thoughts and feelings lie within? I cannot, and will not judge you; but you can and should look at yourself!

The gift of the Holy Spirit can not be bought with money or anything else that man has made. The Holy Spirit can only be given by the power of Jesus!

When you believe and accept the truth of who Jesus is (The son of God), and what he did for us (gave his life on the cross for our sins). Then, and only when we ask God for forgiveness of our sins; will the Holy Spirit be given to us!

Are you just a believer of Jesus Christ? Or are you a born again Christian----- a follower of Jesus Christ?

ARE YOU THE ONE?

(Luke 17:11 through 19)

11) And it came to pass, as he went to Jerusalem that he passed through the midst of Samaria and Galilee.

12) And as he returned into a certain village, there met him ten men that were lepers, which stood afar off:

13) And they lifted up their voices, and said, **Jesus**, *Master, have mercy on us.*

14) And when he saw them, he said unto them, go shew yourselves unto the priests. And it came to pass, that as they went, they were cleansed.

15) And one of them, when he saw that he was healed, turned back, and with a loud voice glorified **God**.

16) And fell down on his face at his feet, giving him thanks: and he was a Samaritan.

17) And **Jesus** *answering said, were there not ten cleansed? But where are the nine?*

18) There are not found that returned to give **glory to God**, *save this stranger.*

19) And he said unto him, Arise, go thy way: thy faith hath made thee whole.

I don't know how this story makes you feel, but it reveals to me just how ungrateful most of the people of this generation have become. Imagine how many **Jesus** heals today, that do not stop and thank him!

How many of us do not worship our almighty **God** on Sunday's, much less everyday! **God** is more than worthy of our praises all day long, and everyday of our life! <u>Do</u> <u>not</u> be one of the nine! Always be that <u>one,</u> that stops and gives thanks for **Gods** grace!

ASK GOD FOR IT!

(Matthew 7:7-8)

Ask, and it shall be given you; seek, and ye shall find; knock, and it shall be opened unto you: for everyone that asketh receiveth; and he that seeketh findeth; and to him that knocketh it shall be opened.

WOW! This is a promise from **Jesus**. He said to ask for your desires, and if they are pure of heart, **God** will deliver them to you. Be very careful what you ask for though. Ask for things of our heavenly father, such as healing of the body and spirit, understanding, courage etc…not things of the world, because he already knows of these needs!

Seek, and ye shall find. **Jesus** says to seek (actively look for), and ye shall find. The best thing that I can think of to seek; is **Jesus** himself! Imagine: we can actually spend private time with our **Lord and Master**!

You can also seek wisdom and knowledge, or even strength of will.

Reading the word of **God** is an excellent way to seek. Praying is also another awesome way.

And then we can knock on the doors of heaven, and they will be opened to us.

If you have already asked **Jesus** to come into your heart; then you also have the **Holy Spirit** living inside of you. Now the power of **God** himself is in your life. Let the **Grace of God** flow through you, so that all may see his glory!

ASTROLOGER'S, STARGAZER'S, AND PROGNOSTICATOR'S

What does *GOD* think about these people?

(Isaiah 47:12 thru 15)

12) Stand now with thine enchantments, and with the multitude of thy sorceries, wherein thou hast laboured from thy youth; if so be thou shalt able to profit, if so be thou mayest prevail.

13) Thou art wearied in the multitude of thy counsels. Let now the astrologers, the stargazers, the monthly prognosticators, stand up, and save thee from these things that shall come upon thee.

14) Behold, they shall be as stubble; the fire shall burn them; they shall not deliver themselves from the power of the flame: there shall not be a coal to warm at, nor fire to sit before it.

15) Thus shall they be unto thee with whom thou hast laboured, even thy merchants, from thy youth: they shall wander every one to his quarter: **none** *shall save thee.*

It's easy to see that *GOD* does not approve of liars and cheats of any kind. These so-called counselors are not the way to see your life, and not your future. If you truly want to know about yourself, then pray and ask the one who made you (*GOD*). He will show you who you are, and who you can become if you will only trust in him!

Behold. I Send You Forth!

(Matthew 10:16)

"Behold, I send you forth as sheep in the midst of wolves; be ye therefore wise as serpents, and harmless as doves."

God does not allow trials and tribulations to enter into our lives to hurt us. Why would he ask his only son ***Jesus*** to give up his life for us, if he wanted us hurt? He loves us more than we can even understand.

The trials and tribulations are so we can grow as Christians, and come closer to our savior ***Jesus***. When we call on him for help, then we are in his presence. When we understand that he is here to guide us through life, then we will call on him more. Some circumstances we are able to handle on our own (by the grace of ***God*** of course). But most of the times we need our savior.

Jesus loves it when we call on him. He loves helping us and showing us the way.

He said we are sheep among wolves because most of the world has chosen to follow someone else. We must be careful not to get caught up in the worldly ways. He tells us to be as wise as serpents. This means we should be willing to humble ourselves to him, knowing that we can not even walk without the grace of ***God***.

And be harmless as doves. When we are born again by asking ***Jesus*** to be our personal savior, he does! He also brings ***the Holy Ghost*** to live inside us. We now have unending power inside us. We are to allow ourselves to be servants to ***God***. Always being careful not to harm his word by our mouth, or by the way we live. Always give the glory to God, and not ourselves.

Call on his name as often as you like. He loves us so much, and wants to hear from us daily. Stay focused on ***Jesus*** and you will always be victorious.

BIRTH IS A BLESSING FROM GOD!

(Psalm 100:3)

3) Know ye that the Lord is God: it is he that hath made us, and not we ourselves; we are his people, and the sheep of his pasture.

God made man in his own image! You are one of his creations! That in itself makes you very special!

I for one thank God that I am one of his children, and not a product of man. I thank my God for sending my brother Jesus to earth, to save me from all my sins. Who could man have possibly sent?

Yes man thinks he now knows how to make mankind. But he is only showing his ignorance, instead of his knowledge. If he were intelligent enough to know that God is real and his Heavenly Father; then he wouldn't waste his time trying to clone a human, or any animal; but spend his life showing God how thankful he is to "Be a Man"... one of Gods children!

Remember that the birth of one of Gods children truly is a blessing, even when we have a child and wasn't planning one! We have absolutely no right to harm or kill these creations! If we do not want these children; we are obligated to bring them into the world, and then find them a safe and loving home!

If we do not want these unexpected miracles, then we need to not have unmarried sex period.

CHRISTIAN'S ARE CONQUEROR'S!

(Romans 8:31)

What shall we say then to these things? If God be for us, who can be against us?

The Apostle Paul asks his brethren in Rome this question.

(Romans 8: 32-33)

32) He that spared not his own son, but delivered him up for us all, how shall he not with him also freely give us all things.

33) Who shall lay anything to the charge of God's elect? It is God that justifieth.

Paul reminds us all that God delivered up his own Son Jesus, to be a sacrifice for us all. And that God is the one in charge, or justifieth.

(Romans 8:34)

Who is he that condemneth? It is Christ that died, yea rather, that is risen again, who is even at the right hand of God, who also maketh intercession for us.

Paul said that Jesus also makes intercession for us. In the same chapter and in the twenty sixth verses, Paul says that the Holy Spirit knows our heart; and makes intercession for us.

Just think; we have the Son of God, and the Spirit of God, making intercession for us. That means that they talk to God for us, and also reveals his word back to us.

You can purely see that we should not worry about anything that this world throws at us.

(Romans 8:35-39)

35) Who hath separated us from the love of Christ? Shall tribulation, or distress, or persecution, or famine, or nakedness, or peril, or sword?

36) As it is written, for thy sake we are killed all the day long; we are accounted as sheep for the slaughter.

37) Nay, in all things we are **more than conquerors through him that loved us**.

38) For I am persuaded that neither death, nor life, nor angels, nor principalities, nor powers, nor things present, nor things to come.

39) Nor height, nor depth nor any other creature, shall be able to separate us from the love of God, which is in Christ Jesus our Lord.

Can you now see how powerful that the sacrifice of Jesus is for us? Those who accept Jesus as their Savior cannot be defeated by anything past, present, or even in the future!

Paul said that even angels can not separate us from the love of God! Paul included angels on purpose; because we know that Satan is a fallen angel.

Look upon your trials and tribulations as a conqueror! And never forget to thank God, the one who made this possible, and of course Jesus and The Holy Ghost too!

COME; SIT WITH ME ON MY THRONE!

(Revelation 3:20-21)

20) Behold, I stand at the door, and knock: if any man hear my voice, and open the door, I will come in to him, and will sup with him, and he with me.

21) To him that overcometh will I grant to **sit with me in my throne**, *even as I also overcame, and am set down with my Father in his throne.*

Jesus told John these important words. Imagine; having an opportunity to be with Jesus on his throne. Sitting right beside God himself! WOW! Can we really sit at the throne?

If you have answered the door of your heart when Jesus called on you, then you have already done what Jesus said would get you into the throne with him.

This is just another blessing that his awesome love has done for us. Love him just as much!

DEATH IS NOT THE END

(Romans 6:3-5)

3) Know ye not, that so many of us were baptized into Jesus Christ were baptized into his death?

4) Therefore we are buried with him by baptism into death: that like as Christ was raised from the dead by the glory of the Father, even so we also should walk in newness of life.

5) For if we have been planted together in the likeness of his death, we shall be also in the likeness of his resurrection.

That is what Jesus did for you in his sacrifice on the cross. Those who believe in him, and accept his atonement for their sins, will be raised from the dead and will live again! Forever!

I am excited that I know this life is merely a learning experience. That this world is only temporary, but the next life will be for ever!

The signs of this world being close to an end are everywhere. Spend the rest of it worshiping, following, and serving Jesus!

He loves you very much! Love him just as much!

DENOMINATION'S ARE FOR MAN; NOT FOR GOD!

There are some people who believe that you have to be a member of a certain church or religion to be saved. But God our father and Jesus his son are not among this group.

(Romans 2:11-16)

11) For there is no respect of persons with God.

12) For as many as have sinned without law shall also perish without law: and as many as have sinned in the law shall be judged by the law;

13) For not the hearers of the law are just before God, but the doers of the law shall be justified.

14) For when the Gentiles, which have not the law, do by nature the things contained in the law, these having not the law, are a law unto themselves:

15) Which shew the work of the law written in their hearts. Their conscience also bearing witness, and their thoughts the means while accusing or excusing one another.

16) In the day when God shall judge the secrets of men by Jesus Christ according to the gospel.

Now you can make reason for anything you want. You can say this, and claim that, but the truth is written for you in the Holy Bible. This is the word and truth of God himself!

He says that he is a respecter of no person, but he will receive all that come to him in the name of Jesus.

If you call on Jesus as a Baptist, then good! If you are a Catholic or Jewish and you call on Jesus, then good! The point is you do not have to be a member of any certain religion. Religion will not get you into Heaven, Grace will!

The only way you can get into Heaven is through the love, and the sacrifice of Jesus Christ. You must accept him as your Lord and Master, and then he will save you from guaranteed Hell!

But knowing the word of God is not enough! You must also obey the word. Satan himself knows the word better than you and I, but he will not obey Gods word. And we know what his final destination is going to be!

Learn Gods words and then live your life by his word and you will receive blessings from the only living Almighty God there is!

DEVIL'S KNOW JESUS!

(Matthew 8:28-29)

And when he was come to the other side into the country of the Ger-ge-senes`, there met him two possessed with devils, coming out of the tombs, exceeding fierce, so that no man might pass by that way, and, behold, they cried out, saying, What have we to do with thee **Jesus, thou son of God?** *Art thou come hither to torment us before the time?*

I want you to notice two things in these verses. First, although these two devils had never met **Jesus,** they recognized him immediately; and called him the **Son Of God.** The other thing they said was art thou come hither to torment us before the time! The devils know that there is a set time for them; when **Jesus, the son of God,** will judge each and every one. They know that their time is only for a short while, and then **Jesus** will torment them!!! The devils know him---do you?

And again in the book of Mark (1:23 thru 25)

And there was in their synagogue a man with an unclean spirit; and he cried out, saying, let us alone; what have we to do with thee, thou **Jesus of Nazareth**? *Art thou come to destroy us? I know thee who thou art, the* **Holy One of God.** *And* **Jesus** *rebuked him, saying, Hold thy peace, and come out of him.*

Again the unclean spirit recognized **Jesus** as **Gods** son, and the one who will torment him.

Then comes the time when **Jesus** cast out many devils into a herd of swine. And they ran into the sea, and the devils perished. This story is found in Mark 5: 1 thru 13.

The result is always the same. They always recognize **Jesus**, and always obey his orders. Devils and Demons are only brave when they come against man; and not the **Son Of God.**

It's your choice! Go through life unprotected and on your own; or choose **Jesus** and his love and strength; and be protected!

FATHER, FORGIVE THEM!

(Luke 23: 34 thru 37)

34) Then said **Jesus**, *Father, forgive them; for they know not what they do. And they parted his raiment, and cast lots.*

35) And the people stood beholding. And the rulers also with them derided him, saying, He saved others; let him save himself, if he be Christ, the chosen of **God.**

36) And the soldiers also mocked him, coming to him, and offering vinegar,

37) And saying, if thou be the king of the Jews, save thyself.

I was reading this passage and I found myself getting very angry at the way they treated my savior; when the Holy Spirit put my thoughts on another scripture.

(Luke 23:27&28)

And there followed him a great company of people, and of women, which also bewailed and lamented him. But **Jesus** *turning unto them said, daughters of Jerusalem,* **weep not for me, but weep for yourselves, and for your children**.

I then realized that even though they had beaten my Lord and Savior beyond recognition; that this is what **Jesus** chose to do! He knew the only way we could be forgiven of our sins, was for him to give himself for a sacrifice to our heavenly father! He also knew that soon he would be going back home to **God**, and the one who didn't understand the importance of his courage, were the ones who were present at his crucifixion. He told the few that wept for him that it was they who needed the weeping! He was soon to be in heaven; and they were still going to be on earth.

Imagine! **Jesus** had just been beaten savagely! He was then forced to carry his own cross up the hill to his own death! But his Love for us is so strong that he prayed and asked **God** to forgive us. How can anyone not accept this incredible savior?

Please tell everyone you know about **Jesus** and his love for all of us!

FATHER'S DAY!

Father is defined as: the male parent or ancestor. June 20th, 2004 is Father's Day. A day we tell our father how much we love and thank him for his love and devotion for us. And if you are blessed to have your Father living, and are able to talk to him, by all means, thank him!

Father is also defined as: The first person of the Holy Trinity. How can we thank our human father, without first thanking our Heavenly Father? Without GOD, there would be no Father's.

(Genesis 1:27)

So GOD created man in his own image, in the image of GOD created he him; male and female created he them.

And GOD said to Honor Thy Father and Thy Mother. He made it one of his ten commandments.

FEAR NOT LITTLE FLOCK!

(Luke 12:29-32)

29) And seek not ye what ye shall eat, or what ye shall drink, neither be ye of doubtful mind.

30) For all these things do the nations of the world seek after: and your **Father** *knoweth that ye have need of these things.*

31) But rather seek ye the **kingdom of God***; and all these things shall be added unto you.*

32) Fear not, little flock; for it is your **Father's** *good pleasure to give you the kingdom.*

This is a powerful message indeed! **Jesus** is telling us that we do not need to worry about the things of this world. We have an almighty **God** that loves us and knows that we have certain needs. **Jesus says to seek the kingdom of God,** and let him take care of our daily needs here on earth; after all...**God** made us!

THE FIRST COMMANDMENT!

(Exodus 20:1 - 3)

And **God** *spake all these words, saying, I am the* **Lord Thy God**, *which have brought thee out of the land of Egypt, out of the house of bondage. Thou shalt have no other Gods before me.*

This was spoken in the Old Testament, by **God** to Moses. He gave him Ten Commandments or laws for the children of Israel to follow. Was the first commandment changed when **Jesus** was born in the New Testament? No!

(Matthew 22:37 & 38)

Jesus *said unto him, "Thou shalt love the* **Lord Thy God** *with all thy heart, and with all thy soul, and with all thy mind. This is the first and great Commandment."*

That was the answer that **Jesus** told a lawyer, when he asked **Jesus** which was the greatest commandment.

Let's look at the First Commandment again. Thou shalt have no other **God's** before me. This means that anything you worship is considered a god. If you worship your husband or wife; then they are gods. If you worship your children; then they are gods. Worship means to honor, or to show reverence for.

So you might think that having other gods is okay, as long as you do not put them before **God.**

But when you know what **God** means by saying before me, he means <u>in</u> <u>his</u> presence! And **God** is everywhere!

So **God** is really saying "Thou shalt have no other gods in period."

By all means love your family! Just do not worship them! Jesus commands that we love everyone, as he loves us. But love and worship are different! So worship God!

"For <u>GOD</u> so loved the world; that he gave his only <u>Begotten Son</u>; that who so-ever believeth in him shall not perish, but will have everlasting Life." John 3:16

For God so loved the world! Understand that God is the creator of all things!

That it was him that <u>gave</u> his only begotten son. Gave, means that our Salvation is a gift from God. We do not have to earn it; and can not earn Salvation with anything that we do. Begotten, means a part of: Jesus came out of God! He was <u>not</u> created like we were. He and God are the same being!

God's love for us is amazing! Jesus was born in this world; lived in this world without sin; and then <u>he</u> <u>gave</u> his own life for those who would believe and accept him! He did all this so that God's created children would not have to perish (To be separated from God for ever). And then, God raised Jesus from the grave so that we also may be raised from our grave; and shall live forever in God's kingdom!

Do you know God's son, *Jesus*? If you do know him as your personal savior, then come worship him with us, at your local Church. If you do not know *Jesus* as your personal savior; they will be glad to help you meet him. He loves you so much and wants to be a part of your life!

If your local church can help you in any way please let them know. Your local church has very loving members and they will be glad to help you. Come worship with us, and you will be glad you did!

FORBID THEM NOT!

(Luke 18:15 thru 17)

15) And they brought unto him also infants, that he would touch them: but when his disciples saw it, they rebuked them.

16) But **Jesus** *called them unto him, and said, suffer little children to come unto me, and forbid them not: for of such is the king-dom of* **God**.

17) Verily I say unto you, whosoever shall not receive the kingdom of **God** *as a little child, shall in no wise enter therein.*

Jesus is telling his disciples and us too, that we must be as little children to receive entrance into **God's** kingdom. What this means is that we must be dependent on our heavenly father for everything! We cannot earn our way into **heaven,** but by the grace of **God**, we can enter. **God** wants us to be a child in his presence, because we are his children. He wants to love us, protect us, guide us in our daily lives, and one day receives us into his home. He knows what is best for us, so ask him for his will, and not our own in everything we do. And never forget to give him thanks!

When you have the creator of all things watching over you, why would you not want to spend time with him and show him you are thankful?

FORSAKE ALL!

(Matthew 19:29-30)

29) And every one that hath forsaken houses, or brethren, or sisters, or father, or mother, or wife, or children, or lands for my name's sake, shall receive an hundredfold, and shall inherit everlasting life.

30) But many that are first shall be last; and the last shall be first.

What **Jesus** is saying is that if you are going to follow him, that you must forsake (relinquish, release) everything else! You are going to have loved ones in your life that will try to keep you focused on things of the world. Remember that the things of this world are only temporary, and the things to come in your next life are going to be permanent!

Where is your heart? What kind of rewards do you want? Are you going to be first or last in heaven? Are you going to heaven or hell? These are questions you have to answer now, not later!

GAYS AND LESBIANS

The Apostle Paul said this about the men and women of Rome that had gone astray in their way of living.

(Romans 1:21-27)

21) Because that, when they knew God, they glorified him not as God, neither were thankful; but became vain in their imaginations, and their foolish heart was darkened.

22) Professing themselves to be wise, they became fools.

23) And changed the glory of the uncorruptible God into an image made like to corruptible man, and to birds, and fourfooted beasts, and creeping things.

24) Wherefore God also gave them up to uncleanness through the lusts of their own hearts, to dishonour their own bodies between themselves:

25) Who changed the truth of God into a lie, and worshipped and served the creature more than the creator, who is blessed forever. A'-Men.

26) For this cause God gave them up unto vile affections: for even their women did change the natural use into that which is against nature.

27) And likewise also the men, leaving the natural use of the woman, burned in their lust one toward another; men with men working that which is unseemly, and receiving in themselves that recompence of their error which was meet.

Paul is addressing the gay and lesbian way of life in Rome. He is revealing God's thoughts about this to the brethren in Rome, in which he hopes to visit soon. It is made very clear that God does not approve of the way that some men and women have changed the way of life that God meant for things to be! And he is not only upset about it, but promises to punish these acts and all unrighteousness.

(Romans 1:29-31)

29) Being filled with all unrighteousness, fornication, wickedness, covetness, maliciousness; full of envy, murder, debate, deceit, malignity; whisperers,

30) Backbiters, haters of God, despiteful, proud, boasters, inventors of evil things, disobedient to parents,

31) Without understanding, covenant breakers, without natural affection, implacable, unmerciful.

I know that I am not perfect. There is a lot of unrighteouness in the world we live in. As we can see in these last three verses, we all have to be careful how we feel about other people. Some people do not seem to take our feelings into consideration. They treat us anyway that is convenient for them! But God says that we are to treat them the way he says; and not the way we think they deserve to be treated.

Whether we agree or do not agree with the way other people choose to live their lives, we must be concerned with our own decisions that directly affect our own lives! We need to make sure that we are pleasing to God in the way we choose to live our lives. Always pray for these and all of

Gods children. If something is not right by Gods word in your life; <u>then</u> <u>change</u>!

Now that I know what God does not like, I see that I have a lot of work within myself to do. If you want to be blessed by God, and not punished; then maybe you had better get to work on yourself as well! I am going to let God help me change the things that are not right in his will! I want his love and blessings!

GO AHEAD AND TELL LIES ABOUT ME; AND I WILL THANK YOU!

(Matthew 5:11)

11) Blessed are ye, when men shall revile you, and persecute you, and shall say all manner of evil against you falsely, **for my sake.**

(Matthew 5:12)

12) Rejoice, and be exceeding glad: for great is your reward in heaven: for so persecuted they the prophets which were before you.

A close member in the family told my wife that the only reason that I wanted an office in my Church was so that I could receive praise from the other members. I know, and more importantly **God knows**, that this is no more than a lie sent from Satan. Instead of feeling fear that someone may believe this lie, I am giving thanks to our **God in Heaven**, because he will receive glory from this. I thank him for letting me be a part of his family. Let other's tell lies about you too, and be exceeding glad. Thank you **God!**

Revile:

1) Subject to verbal use
2) To use abusive language

Persecute:

1) To cause to suffer because of belief
2) To harass in a manner designed to injure, grieve, or afflict

GOD FORGIVES!

Who said that **God** forgives us of our sins? **God did!** He told Ezekiel to go and tell Israel to turn aside from their iniquities, and they would live.

(Ezekiel 18:21)

21) But if the wicked will turn from all his sins that he hath committed, and keep all my statutes, and do that which is lawful and right, he shall surely live, he shall not die.

(Ezekiel 18:27)

27) Again, when the wicked man turneth away from his wickedness that he hath committed, and doeth that which is lawful and right, he shall save his soul alive."

Our heavenly father wants each one of us to live!

(Ezekiel 18:32)

32) For I have no pleasure in the death of him that dieth, saith the **Lord God**: *wherefore turn yourselves, and live ye.*

God loves us and only wants us to love him. We must be obedient to him, and his laws. The ways of man only confuse us, and take us further away from the love and comfort of our heavenly father. Forget the pleasures of the world, which fade quickly; and receive the pleasures of **God**, which will last forever!

GOD AND MAMMON!

(Luke 16:13)

13) No servant can serve two masters: for either he will hate the one, and love the other; or else he will hold to the one, and despise the other. Ye cannot serve **God** *and Mammon.*

Mammon: Riches regarded as an evil influence and ignoble goal; Worldliness.

This statement from **Jesus** is self explanatory. If we are to truly worship our Savior, then we must quit trying to have the best things that man has to offer. We can either serve **Jesus,** by faithfully following him daily; not only on Sundays and Wednesday nights, or we can serve ourselves and the riches of this world. One is temporary and fading fast, while the other is going to last for eternity! It is however---your choice! Make the right one.

GOD, HOW DO I WORSHIP THEE?

(John 4:23 - 24)

But the hour cometh, and now is, when the true worshippers shall worship **the Father** *in spirit and truth: for* **the Father** *seeketh such to worship him.* **God** *is a spirit: and they that worship him must worship him in spirit and in truth.*

Jesus told the woman of Samaria to worship his Father; you do so in spirit, and in truth. She perceived Jesus as a prophet. She said that there was to come a messiah, who would speak of all things. Jesus then told her that he was the one she was looking for. If we are to worship God; then we must first worship his son Jesus!

GOD'S DAY

(Deuteronomy 5:12-14)

12) Keep the sabbath day to sanctify it, as the ***Lord Thy God*** *hath commanded thee.*

13) Six days thou shalt labour, and do all thy work:

14) But the seventh day is the sabbath of the ***Lord Thy God****; in it thou shalt not do any work, thou, nor thy son, nor thy daughter, nor thy manservant, nor thy maidservant, nor thine ox, nor thine ass, nor any of thy cattle, nor thy stranger that is within thy gates; that they may rest as well as thou.*

Keep the sabbath day, to sanctify it. This is an order from ***GOD*** himself. It simply means that the sabbath (which is to rest from all work on the seventh day of the week) is to be sanctified. Sanctify means: to set apart to a sacred purpose, or to religious use: to free from sin (Purify). Simply put ***GOD*** demands that we give him praise every seven days. But we should treat every day of the week as a day of worship to him. He really is worthy of all that we have!

It was important enough to God, that he made it one of his Ten Commandments.

GOD'S PROTECTION

(Exodus 17:8-15)

8) Then came Am`-a-lek, and fought with Israel in Reph`-i-dim.

9) And Moses said unto Joshua, choose us out men, and go out, fight with Am`-a-lek: tomorrow I will stand on the top of the hill with the rod of God in my hand.

10) So Joshua did as Moses had said to him and fought with Am`-a-lek: and Moses, Aaron, and Hur went up to the top of the hill.

11) And it came to pass, when Moses held up his hand, that Israel prevailed: and when he let down his hand, Am`-a-lek prevailed.

12) But Moses` hands were heavy; and they took a stone, and put it under him, and he sat thereon; and Aaron and Hur stayed up his hands, the one on the one side, and the other on the other side; and his hands were steady until the going down of the sun.

13) And Joshua discomfited Am`-a-lek and his people with the edge of the sword.

14) And the Lord said unto Moses, write this for a memorial in a book, and rehearse it in the ears of Joshua: for I will utterly put out the rememberence of Am`-a-lek from under the heaven.

15) And Moses built an alter, and called the name of it Je-ho`-vah-nis`-si:

This is a powerful story, and a small example of God's almighty power. As long as Moses held up the rod of God the Israelites were winning the battle; but when his hands became tired and he lowered the rod of God; the Am`aleks started winning! So without the power of God and his direction, the Israelites would have been defeated that day.

We too can defeat our trials and tribulations just as the Israelites did. Because we are God's children also! And if we ask God for his help, and then wait on his direction, we will then be victorious.

God then told Moses to write down the victory and share it with Joshua. He wanted Joshua to know that it was God that defeated the Am`alek's that day; and not Joshua. When God defeats your trials and tribulations, make sure that you remember that it was him, and not you that have the power. And always be sure to thank God for everything!

GOD'S WORD IS POWERFUL!

(John 1:1)

1) In the beginning was the word, and the word was with **God**, *and the word was* **God**.

John understood that the very beginning of mankind was through the word of **God**, and that **God** was the one who gave man **God's** word. He also knew how powerful the word is.

(Genesis 1:1 thru 3)

In the beginning **God** *created the heaven and the earth. And the earth was without form, and void; and darkness was upon the face of the deep. And the* **Spirit of God** *moved upon the face of the waters. And* **God** **said**, *Let there be light: and there was light.*

God spoke the earth into existence! He created the world as we know it; with his voice! He created an entire world with just his word! **God** *said let there be light; and there was light.*

Continue to read the first chapters of Genesis, and you will read that **God** *said let there be a firmament in the midst of the waters, and let it divide the waters from the waters. (Genesis 1:6)*

If you continue to read The Bible; you will find that every time **God** did something, he spoke it. **God's word** is so powerful; that not even **God** will disobey it. When he told Adam and Eve that to eat of the tree of Knowledge of good and evil would mean certain death; he meant it. We know that they eventually they did eat of the tree, and they and all of mankind have to pay the price of death.

Later **God** had a change of heart, and wanted man to come and live with him in heaven, but would not go against his own word. That would have made him a liar!

So he sent his only begotten son **Jesus** to the world to die on the cross and pay the price of death for us (sin); so that with **Jesus'** victory over death we could now be free from sin. And when **God raised Jesus** from the grave, he opened the door to heaven for all of us to go with him. But **Jesus** is the only one who can take us home to heaven; there is no other way. You see how powerful that **Gods word is?**

GREAT FEAR;
IS GREAT!

(Isaiah 51:12&13)

I, even I, am he that comforteth you: who art thou, that thou shouldest be afraid of a man that shall die, and of the son of man which shall be made of grass; and forgetest the **Lord thy maker**, *that hath stretched forth the heavens, and laid the foundations of the earth; and hast feared continually every day because of the fury of the oppressor, as if he were ready to destroy? And where is the fury of the oppressor?*

God asks the question of why be afraid of men, when we know that one day they too will die, but do not fear him (The Almighty creator of the entire world?)

(Matthew 10:28)

And fear not them which kill the body, but are not able to kill the soul: but rather fear him which is able to destroy both soul and body in hell.

And again in the book of Matthew, **Jesus** also reminds us that we should not fear man; because man can only hurt our mortal body (that is here for only a short time). Man can do nothing to our immortal soul (that will be around for ever). But our **Lord** can destroy both, in hell!

So how can we go through life and not have any fear towards man?

(Hebrews 13:6)

"So that we may boldly say, The **Lord** *is my helper, and I will not fear what man shall do unto me."*

If we walk with **Jesus** every day, we have no reason to fear any man!

(Isaiah 41:13)

For **I the Lord thy God** *will hold thy right hand, saying unto thee, Fear not;* **I** *will help thee.*

What is fear? Fear: The agitated feeling aroused by awareness of actual or threatening danger. Why do we have fear?

(Deuteronomy 6:2)

That thou mightest fear **The Lord thy God**, *to keep all his statues and his commandments; which* **I** *command thee, thou, and thy son, and thy son's son, all the days of thy life; that thy days may be prolonged.*

(Deuteronomy 10:20)

Thou shalt fear the **Lord thy God***; him shalt thou serve, and to him shalt thou cleave, and sware by his name.*

When you have fear of someone; you want to please that person, so that their anger is not directed towards you. You recognize that, that person has the ability to make your life miserable. You show that person respect, again to avoid their anger. You might also even try to avoid that person. So fear has some good qualities to it. Fear teaches us how to be humble. Fear teaches us how to have, and show respect. But to avoid someone because we are afraid of them is cowardness; and **God** did not put that in his children.

(2nd Timothy 1:7)

For **God** *hath not given us* **The Spirit** *of fear, but of Power, and of Love, and of a Sound Mind.*

(Proverbs 1:33)

"But whoso harkeneth unto me shall dwell safely, and shall be quiet from fear of evil."

Now we know what fear is. We also know what fear does. And we know who to give our fear to. The fear you have, is a really special fear. If you are a born again Child **of God,** Our fear makes us fear **God**! We want to please him! We want his favor! We show our **God** love, respect, honor, praise, and give him glory in the way that we live! We are fearful of **God**, but instead of avoiding him, we seek him. We accept his most special gift, his only begotten son **Jesus**, as our **Lord** and **Master**, who saved us from our sins and opened the door to heaven. The greater your fear of **God**, the better you will serve him. So again I say that great fear...... is great!

THE GREATEST COMMANDMENT!

(Matthew 22:36 thru 40)

36) Master, which is the great commandment in the law?

37) ***Jesus*** *said unto him, "Thou shalt Love the* **Lord** *Thy* **God** *with All Thy Heart, and with All Thy Soul, and with All Thy Mind.*

38) This Is the First And Great Commandment.

39) And the second is like unto it, Thou Shalt Love Thy Neighbor as Thyself."

40) On these two Commandments hang all the Law and the prophets.

If you truly wish to improve on your relationship with ***Jesus***; then you must live by these two commandments. Of course all

Of ***God's*** commandments are important; but these are so important, that these are what ***Jesus*** answered the lawyer with.

I do not know about you, but I have some more work to do!

HAVE YOU BEEN CHOSEN?

If you are saved by the grace of God, and the sacrifice of Jesus; then you need to know that you were chosen by God. He knew you long before you were saved.

(Romans 8:28-30)

28) And we know that all things work together for good to them that love God, to them who are called according to his purpose.

29) For whom he did foreknow; he also did predestinate to be conformed to the image of his Son, that he might be the firstborn among many brethren.

Predestinate: To foreordain by divine decree or purpose.

God chose you to be in the image of Jesus! That you were chosen to be in his own family! Wow! God himself wants you to be one of his children! How blessed can one person get! To be free from death and sin, and not be condemned to Hell! Not only to be free, but to have the only living God to watch over you day and night, giving you his love and protection. Having his grace upon you!

30) Moreover whom he did predestinate, them he also called: and whom he called, them he also justified: and whom he justified, them he also glorified.

God has not only called you to his kingdom, but wants you to be a messenger. There are other children that he has chosen for his own, and he wants us to tell them. We do not know who God has chosen, but he does. Spread the great news about what God has done for you, and maybe someone else you talk to will be a chosen one too.

HOLY BULL?

It was July 17, 2004. I was playing a game on the internet while listening to the 6:00 p.m. news. They told a story about a Holy Bull? In Cambodia there is a farmer that claims his wife, who was licked by this bull, suddenly became healed from her chronic back pain. The report goes on to say that there are several local people who are lined up to spend a moment with this particular bull.

They believe that the bull has healing power. As a Christian the story only reinforces the truth of what

God says about Israel to Jeremiah. It would also pertain to his children of today.

(Jeremiah 5:21)

Hear now this, O foolish people, and without under-standing; which have eyes, and see not; which have ears, and hear not:

(Jeremiah 5:22)

Fear ye not me? saith the ***Lord****: will ye not tremble at my presence, which have placed the sand for the bound of the sea by a perpetual decree, that it cannot pass it: and though the waves thereof toss themselves, yet can they not prevail; though they roar, yet can they not pass over it?*

God tells Jeremiah the prophet that his chosen people have yet again turned to evil ways. He tells of how we as Sinner's are looking for the things of the world to supply our needs, and wants. How many times does ***God*** have to save us?

Why does he have to continually get our attention? He is an almighty and powerful Spirit; who loves us more than we could understand. But he is also the Maker of all things; and more than deserves our love and respect. See with your eyes, and hear with your ears!

HONOR THY FATHER AND THY MOTHER! (GOD'S FIFTH COMMANDMENT)

(Exodus 20:12)

Honour thy father and thy mother; that thy days may be long upon the land which the **Lord Thy God** *giveth thee.*

Honor: High regard, respect, or esteem.

God says that we are to show our parents respect. Give them high regard. But what if one or both of them do something that is unworthy of honor? What if they make some bad choices? Does **God** want us to honor them then? -----Absolutely!

Our parents are on this earth just as we are. They were also born into a sinful world, and they too will sin!

God's Commandment was not "Be the judge of your father and mother." Do not honor their sins and mistakes! We are allowed to disagree with bad decisions! We are to follow our parents in love and respect. This is also a lesson that we will use for eternity, if we have accepted **God's** son **Jesus** as our Savior. How are we going to love and respect **Jesus**, if we have not been loving and respecting our parents? We won't know how if we haven't already been practicing these feelings on them. We also need to practice forgiving. So honor your parents as your parents.

And forgive them if they make a bad decision from time to time. **And always honor God, Jesus, and the Holy Ghost!**

HOPE, WHAT IS IT?

Hope: To desire with expectation of fulfillment. To wish; want.

(Romans 8: 24 and 25)

24) For we are saved by hope: but hope that is seen is not hope: for what a man seeth, why doth he yet hope for?

25) But if hope for that we see not, then do we with patience wait for it.

Paul said it about as well as anyone can say what hope is. If we can see something, and then want it, it is not hope but lust or desire. Rather we hope for the things that cannot be seen.

Salvation is something that cannot be seen, but the results of Salvation can be seen! Our Lord says that we become a new creation, and you can truly see the change in someone who has been born again.

What do you hope for? What do you desire to have, and cannot see? My hope is to be with my Savior for eternity! I also hope for his blessings for my family, and yours.

THE HOUSE OF GOD!

(Haggai 2:7-9)

7) And I will shake all nations, and the desire of all nations shall come: and I will fill this house with Glory, saith the **Lord of hosts**.

8) The silver is mine, and the gold is mine, saith the **Lord of hosts.**

9) The Glory of this latter house shall be greater

than of the former, saith the **Lord of hosts***: and in this place will I give Peace, saith the* **Lord of hosts.**

Through the voice of the prophet Haggai, **God** speaks of the Temple that he is having them build. **God** said that this Temple is greater in his eyes than silver and gold, which are also his. Simply put, this means that **God** will receive glory in his temples and churches; and not from the riches of the world.

That does not mean that **God** is only found in churches. **God** is indeed everywhere; but when you go to one of his houses, you go to learn about him, or to praise him! Either way, you are focusing on him, and he receives glory!

He loves us so much, and only wants us to spend quality time with him. So go to his house on every opportunity that you can, and always go for him!

HOW DOES GOD FEEL WHEN I ACCEPT HIS SON JESUS?

There is a story that Jesus tells his followers in the book of Luke 15: 10 thru 32.

10) Likewise, I say unto you, there is joy in the presence of the angels of God over one sinner that repenteth.

11) And he said," A certain man had two sons:

12) And the younger of them said to his father, Father, give me the portion of goods that falleth me. And he divided unto them his living.

13) And not many days after the younger son gathered all together, and took his journey into a far country, and there wasted his substance with riotious living.

14) And when he had spent all, there arose a mighty famine in that land; and he began to be in want.

15) And he went and joined himself to a citizen of that country; and he sent him into his fields to feed swine.

16) And he would fain have filled his belly with the husks that the swine did eat: and no man gave unto him.

17) And when he came unto himself, he said, How many hired servants of my father's have bread enough and to spare, and I perish with hunger!

18) I will arise and go to my father, and will say unto him, Father; I have sinned against heaven, and before thee.

19) And am no more worthy to be called thy son: make me as one of the hired servants.

20) And he arose, and came to his father. But when he was yet a great way off, his father saw him, and had compassion, and ran, and fell on his neck, and kissed him.

21) And the son said unto him, Father, I have sinned against heaven, and in thy sight, and am no more worthy to be called thy son.

22) But the father said to his servants, Bring forth the best robe, and put it on him; and put a ring on his hand, and shoes on his feet:

23) And bring hither the fatted calf, and kill it; and let us eat, and be merry:

24) For this my son was dead, and is alive again; he was lost, and is found. And they began to be merry.

25) Now his older son was in the field: and as he came and drew nigh to the house, he heard musick and dancing.

26) And he called one of his servants, and asked what these things meant.

27) And he said unto him, Thy brother is come; and thy father hath killed the fatted calf, because he hath received him safe and sound.

28) And he was angry, and would not go in: therefore came his father out, and intreated him.

29) And he answering said to his father, Lo, these many years do I serve thee, neither transgressed I at any time thy commandment: and yet thou never gavest me a kid, that I might make merry with my friends:

30) But as soon as this thy son was come, which had devoured thy living with harlots, thou hast killed for him the fatted calf.

31) And he said unto him, **Son, thou art with me, and all I have is thine.**

32) It was meet that we should make merry, and be glad: **for this thy brother was dead, and is alive again; and was lost, and is found.**

This story is a perfect example of how easy salvation is to receive! If we will just go to Jesus, and tell him that we want him to forgive us for our sins, and ask him to be our Lord and Savior; then all the angels along with God our Heavenly Father, will celebrate our birth into the kingdom of God. And we will become joint heirs with Jesus. Jesus will then tell us that all he has is ours also. WOW! WHAT A SAVIOR!

HUMBLE YOURSELF!

(Matthew 18:1-4)

*At the same time came the disciples unto **Jesus** saying, "Who is the greatest in the kingdom of **Heaven**?" And **Jesus** called a little child unto him, and set him in the midst of them, and said," Verily I say unto you, except ye be converted, and become as little children; ye shall not enter into the kingdom of **Heaven**." Whosoever therefore shall humble himself as this little child; the same is greatest in the kingdom of **Heaven**."*

Humble: 1) Not proud, or arrogant, or assertive
2) Reflecting, expressing, or offered in Spirit of remission!

Is ***Jesus*** saying that we must become 3 or 4 years old again? What about 7 or 8 years old? Our age has nothing to do with what ***Jesus*** is telling his disciples. *J*esus is not talking about our bodies at all, but our Spirit must be converted. We must believe that ***Jesus*** is who he says he is (The Son of ***God)***; and that he died on the cross to save us from our sins. We must surrender ourselves to him in love. We must want to change our old ways and be willing to learn his ways. ***God*** becomes our father and we become his child. We truly are children again. If you have already surrendered yourself to ***Jesus***, then you are great in the kingdom of Heaven! If not, then ***Jesus*** has made room for you there. Do not wait another moment.

I AM YOUR PEACE

"These things **I** *have spoken unto you, that* **in me** *ye might have peace. In the world ye shall have tribulation: but be of good cheer;* **I** *have overcome the world."*

(John 16:33)

I am so very thankful that we have a **Lord** and **Savior** who not only defeated the world that we live in; but is willing to help get us through it also!

I surely struggle with my tribulations, and now call on **Jesus** every time. I can not imagine anyone trying to go through this world without **him**. There are a lot of people that try though. The proof is in their results.

I am a living example myself. I have suffered defeats and many disappointments. And every time I stop and think about those times, I realize that those were also the times that I made decisions on my own, and did not wait on **Jesus** to help me. Ask **Jesus** to help you with all of your tribulations; and then wait on him!

I PROMISE!

Everyone makes promises, and most of the time we come through with those promises. God makes promises also, and never falls short! Even the father of many nations fell short in his promise to trust God.

(Genesis 12:1-3)

1) Now the Lord had said unto Abram, Get thee out of thy country, and from thy kindred, and from thy fathers house, unto a land that I will shew thee:

2) And I will make of thee a great nation, and I will bless thee, and make thy name great; and thou shalt be a blessing:

3) And I will bless them that bless thee, and curse them that curseth thee; and in thee shall all families of earth be blessed.

Here is a perfect example of a promise from God. He promises Abram that if he will leave his home, and go to a land that he will show him; in return for his obedience he will make Abram the father of many nations. God also promised to bless anyone that blessed Abram, and curse anyone that cursed him. In other words, anyone messing with Abram would answer to God!

(Genesis 12:6-7)

6) And Abram passed through the land unto the place of Si'-chem, unto the plain of Mo'-reh. And the Ca'-naan-ite was then in the land.

7) And the Lord appeared unto Abram, and said, Unto thy seed will I give this land: and there builded he an alter unto the Lord, who appeared unto him.

Now, there can not be any doubt in Abram's mind that God has not forsaken him. God appears to Abram and promises to give his children the land of the Ca'-naan-ite's. So Abram continues south on his journey towards Egypt.

(Genesis 12:11-13)

11) And it came to pass, when he was come near to enter into Egypt, that he said unto Sa'-rai his wife, behold now, I know that thou art a fair woman to look upon:

12) Therefore it shall come to pass, when the Egyptians shall see thee, that they shall say, this is thy wife: and they will kill me, but they will save thee alive,

13) Say I pray thee, that thou art my sister: that it may be well with me for thy sake; and my soul shall live because of thee:

This shows me just how fragile we humans really are! The father of many nations, Abram, has fallen into the flesh, and fearing for his very life. He has forgotten that our Almighty God is with him!

(Genesis 12:14-16)

14) And it came to pass, that when Abram was come into Egypt, the Egyptians beheld the woman that she was very fair.

15) The princes also of Pharoh saw her, and commended her before Pharoh: and the woman was taken into Pharoh's house.

16) And he entreated Abram well for her sake: and he had sheep, and oxen, and he asses, and menservants, and maidservants, and she asses, and camels.

Remember at the beginning, the promise that God had promised to bless Abram. Now, even that Abram had made a decision without talking to God, he still blessed him. See how even when we are not focused on God, he is still focused on us!

(Genesis 12:17-20)

17) And the Lord plagued Pharoh and his house with great plagues because of Sa'-rai Abram's wife.

18) And Pharoh called Abram, and said, what is this that thou hast done unto me? Why didst thou not tell me that she was thy wife?

19) Why saidst thou, she is my sister? So I might have taken her to me to wife: now therefore behold thy wife, take her, and go thy way.

20) And Pharoh commanded his men concerning him: and they sent him away, and his wife, and all that he had.

Now what do you suppose would have happened if Abram had prayed, and talked to God, and told him about his concerns before going into Egypt? What do you think God might have done? God, even though Abram did not ask, continued to protect Abram and his company, just as he had promised to do!

Sometimes we make bad choices ourselves, without talking to God first. But we can be sure that he has not left our side, just as he has promised us! You can believe and know that God will never fall short of his promises.

I AM NOT ASHAMED!

If I try to tell someone, even a member of my family about Jesus; then they will make fun of me and get mad at me! They might not even want to see me anymore! What do you say Lord?

(Luke 21: 16-18)

"And ye shall be betrayed both by parents, and brethren, and kinsfolks, and friends; and some of you shall they cause to be put to death. And ye shall be hated of all men for my names sake. But there shall not an hair of your head perish. In your patience posses ye your souls."

Now I ask you; are you a born again Christian? Have you truly accepted Jesus as your Savior? Are you afraid to say Jesus' name out loud because someone might get mad?

I have been told by a family member that there is a proper place and time for the word of God! I agree, and that is all the time, day and night, everyday! My boss told me that the job sight is not a place for the Lord. I told him that my God goes with me everywhere I go! After all – He lives inside of me in the form of the Holy Spirit!

Jesus said that if you are ashamed of him in the face of men, then he will be ashamed of you in front of his father. You may not like me talking of Jesus in front of you, but I will not be ashamed of my Savior in front of you or anybody else! You need Jesus just as much as I do, but you may not love him as much as I do! Are you ashamed?

I AM NOT THAT BAD!

I haven't killed anyone. I haven't stolen anything. I haven't cheated anyone, or cussed, or anything else!

I must be a pretty good person. Far better than the Prostitute or the homeless bums. I know that I am better than the crooked Officials and Lawyers!

(Luke 18: 10 thru 14)

10) Two men went up into the temple to pray; the one a Pharisee, and the other a publican.

11) The Pharisee stood and prayed thus with himself,

God, *I thank thee, that I am not as other men are, extortioners, unjust, adulterers, or even as this publican.*

12) I fast twice in the week; I give tithes of all that I possess.

13) And the publican, standing afar off, would not lift up so much as his eyes unto heaven, but smote upon his breast, saying, **God** *be merciful to me a sinner.*

14) I tell you, this man went down to his house justified rather than the other: for every one that exalteth himself shall be abased: and he that humbleth himself shall be exalted.

When you look into the mirror, what kind of person do you see? How would you describe yourself? Are you a good person, or are you a sinner? Do you see yourself as **Jesus** sees you? Pray and ask **Jesus** and find out! Do you think you are better than the publican, or the drunk, or the prostitute?

I AM THE DOOR!

(John 9:7-9)

7) Then said Jesus unto them again, "Verily, verily, I say unto you, I am the door of the sheep.

8) All that ever came before me were thieves and robbers: but the sheep did not hear them.

9) I am the door: by me if any man enter in, he shall be saved, and shall go in and out, and find pasture."

I am so thankful to God for knowing that Jesus truly is my shepherd. I know where my place in life is now, and also where I am going to spend eternity. I am both thrilled with the blessing from God to have his son as my shepherd, and am extremely sad that all God's children are not in the pasture of Jesus.

Some are in the pasture with the wolf (Satan), and will suffer a horrible fate very soon. There is still time for these sheep to escape their fate, if they will only call out to Jesus. He will rescue them all if they will only ask him to.

Whose pasture are you in? What shepherd is guarding your life? Is it Jesus or the Big Bad Devil? Look at the gate of your life!

I DO NOT UNDERSTAND THIS!

Are there things in your life that you do not understand? Are situations getting out of hand in your opinion? Are you frustrated because you have the answers, but when you do make a decision; it does not solve the problem?

What is frustration?

Frustration: A deep chronic sense or state of insecurity and dissatisfaction arising from unresolved problems or unfulfilled needs.

What can we do about our frustration? In the book of Proverbs we find our answer.

(Proverbs 3:5)

Trust in the Lord with all thine heart; *and lean not unto thine own understanding.*

God sent his only begotten son **Jesus** to save us from our sins; but also to save us from being alone in our lives in making decisions. He knows everything about us and our circumstances. Trust in him to take care of all your needs. He really does have all the answers!

JESUS AND GOD ARE ONE!

Where in the Bible does it say that Jesus is God? What does Emanuel mean? Why does Jesus say that we are his when we were created by God?

(John 10:27 thru 30)

27) My sheep hear my voice, and I know them, and they follow me;

28) And I give unto them eternal life; and they shall never perish; neither shall any man pluck them out of my hand.

29) My Father, which gave them me, is greater then all; and no man is able to pluck them out of my Father's hand.

30) **I and my Father are one.**

And again in one of his final prayers to God; Jesus is praying for those that believe in his word.

(John 17:11)

"And now I am no more in the world; but these are in the world, and I come to thee. Holy Father, keep through thine own name those whose thou hast given me that they may be one, as we are."

This word comes from the greatest witness that has ever walked this planet, Jesus! Emanuel means God with us.

Now you know where in the Bible it says that Jesus and God are one in the same. And you know who said it, Jesus did! You can tell everyone boldly that we are Jesus sheep! And that no man can take us away from our shepherd.

If you do not know the love of Jesus for yourself, then get down on your knees and ask him to make himself known to your heart. Ask him to be your Savior! You will then receive the only one who can and will deliver you from evil and damnation.

And he will never leave you! Nor forsake you!

JESUS BLESSES SIMON

(Luke 5:1 - 10)

1) And it came to pass, that, as the people pressed upon **him** *to hear the word of* **God**, *he stood by the lake of Gen-nes`-a-ret.*

2) And saw two ships standing by the lake; but the fisherman were gone out of them, and were washing their nets.

3) And **he** *entered into one of the ships, which was Simon's, and prayed him that he would thrust out a little from the land. And* **he** *sat down, and taught the people out of the ship.*

4) Now when **he** *had left speaking,* **he** *said unto Simon, "Launch out into the deep, and let down your nets for a draught."*

5) And Simon answering said unto **him**, *Master, we have toiled all the night, and have taken nothing: nevertheless at thy word I will let down the net.*

6) And when they had this done, they inclosed a great multitude of fishes; and their net brake.

7) And they beckoned unto their partners, which were in the other ship, that they should come and help them. And they came, and filled both the ships, so that they began to sink.

8) When Simon Peter saw it, he fell down at **Jesus's** *knees, saying, depart from me; for I am a sinful man,* **O Lord**.

9) For he was astonished, and all that were with him, at the draught of the fishes which they had taken:

10) And so was also James, and John, the sons of Zeb`-e-dee, which were partners with Simon, "Fear not; from henceforth thou shalt catch men."

This is only one of **Jesus'** amazing stories.

Try and put yourself in Simon's place. Here he and his crew come into shore after an all night fishing trip. They had not even caught any fish. They had to be tired, because fishing for a living was extremely hard work. Probably angered somewhat because no-one was going to make any money and they still had to clean all their nets. Now what else could happen?

Along comes a man named **Jesus**. And he asks Simon to take **him** out a little bit, so he could teach the multitude.

What do you think you would do? But Simon goes ahead with **Jesus'** request. He was obviously curious about what **Jesus** had in mind, and wanted to hear what **Jesus** had to say. What do you think Simon's tired crew was thinking?

Not only does **Jesus** tell Simon to then go into deep water, but tells him also to have his men drop their nets again. They just got done cleaning them, which is no easy task. Now what do you believe they were thinking?

But because they obey **Jesus**, they are rewarded in a way that can only be called a miracle! That is what men call an impossible deed, for a man to accomplish.

Not only is there so much fish for the nets to hold without breaking; but there are so many fish that two ships are about to sink from the weight of all the fish.

Peter knows the proper thing to do. He immediately gets down on his knees in front of **Jesus, and praises him!** Peter knows where the fish came from, and so did everyone else that was there. What if you had been a passenger on either ship; how do you think you would have reacted?

Would you be on your knees in front of **Jesus**, or would you think that Simon is the luckiest person on the face of the earth?

Remember that **Jesus** doesn't have need of luck, because **he** uses power. Do not answer these questions to me, but rather tell your answers to **Jesus!**

THE KINGDOM IS PREACHED!

(Luke 16:16)

"The law and the prophets were until John: since that time the Kingdom of ***God*** *is preached, and every man presseth into it."*

Pressing: Demanding immediate attention.

Jesus tells us that the laws of the Old Testament are still the laws of today. But the laws will not get you into Heaven! Only by receiving **Jesus** as your Savior can you live for eternity in the Kingdom Of **God**.

And **Jesus** also says that the message of Salvation will be preached! If you are not going to church, then how will you hear **Gods** words?

And never forget to talk with **Jesus** daily! Prayer is the powerful way you build a relationship with our Lord and Master.

LET THEM GROW TOGETHER!

In a parable spoke by Jesus in the thirteenth chapter in Matthew; he tells of a man who had his workers plant good seed in his pasture. While night fell, in darkness his enemy planted tares in the same pasture.

When the seed and tares started to grow, the workers noticed the tares, and asked the owner what he wished them to do. And the answer is found in Matthew 13:30.

Jesus said, Let them grow together until the harvest: and in the time of the harvest I will say to the reapers, gather ye together first the tares, and bind them in bundles to burn them: but gather the wheat into my barn.

There is both super sweet joy, and terrible tragedy in this news. Of course as a born again Christian the news brings great joy! But the terrible tragedy is that not everyone will be going to heaven. A lot of Gods creations will be heading for horrible torture. We need to do all we can now to tell everyone how they can avoid this tragedy. No-one needs to go to hell and suffer. Tell someone about Jesus, and his ability to save them from certain destruction.

LOVE THY GOD!

(Mark 12:30)

30) And thou shalt love the **Lord thy God** *with all thy heart, and with all thy soul, and with all thy mind, and with all thy strength; this is the first commandment.*

Jesus said that we are to show our heavenly father all of the love that is in us. All the love that we have in our hearts (ones inner most character, feelings, or inclination). All the love that we have in our souls (a person's total self). All the love we have in our minds ;(the elements in an individual that feels, perceives, thinks, wills, and especially reasons). And even all the love that we carry in our strength (the physical ability of each individual).

If we are believers in **Jesus Christ**; then we are already believer's in **God**; his father. And we also know that **God** made us and everything else around us. We should not have to be reminded that we are to love the only living **God** there is. But unfortunately, there are some of us that do have to be reminded. Give **God** all your love and see how much better you feel. Besides; he deserves and demands your love! **So Praise God! And remember, He's our Father too!**

MAY I WASH YOUR FEET?

(John 13: 4 -17)

4) He riseth from supper, and laid aside his garments; and took a towel, and girded himself.

5) After that he poureth water into a bason, and began to wash the desciples' feet, and to wipe them with the towel wherewith he was girded.

6) Then cometh he to Simon Peter; and Peter saith unto him, Lord, dost thou wash my feet?

7) Jesus answered and said unto him, what I do thou knowest not now; but thou shalt know hereafter.

8) Peter saith unto him, Thou shalt never wash my feet. Jesus answered him, If I wash thee not, thou hast no part of me.

9) Simon Peter saith unto him, Lord, not my feet only, but also my hands and my head.

10) Jesus saith to him, "He that is washed needeth not save to wash his feet, but is clean every whit: and ye are clean, but not all.

11) For he knew who should betray him; therefore said he, Ye are not all clean.

12) So after he had washed their feet, and had taken his garments, and was set down again, he said unto them, Know ye what I have done to you?

13) Ye call me Master and Lord: and ye say well; for so I am.

14) If I then, your Lord and Master, have washed your feet; ye also ought to wash one another's feet.

15) "For I have given you an example that ye should do as I have done to you.

16) Verily, verily, I say unto you, the servant is not greater than his Lord; neither he that is sent is greater than he that sent him.

17) If ye know these things, happy are ye if ye do them.

The feet are the dirtiest part of the body, beside the mouth. Here Jesus showed the Disciples and us too, that he was willing to wash their feet. He showed us all that he was, our servant. He then soon after died on the cross for our sins, so we would not have to! He also told them that to call him Lord and Master was a wise thing to do, because he is. He showed us that the Lord and

Master was willing to do whatever he had to- for our life! Then he left the Commandment for us to do the same thing for each other. Can I wash your feet? I want to be like my Lord and Master! I pray that the Holy Spirit will always show me how to be obedient to my Master. Do you want to be like Jesus? Do your actions prove this? Or are <u>your</u> actions from another Master!

MEMORIAL'S

Is it alright to have a memorial for a loved one, or someone else that performed wisely? What does Jesus say about the subject?

(Matthew 26: 6-13)

6) Now when **Jesus** *was in Beth`-a-ny, in the house of Simon the leper,*

7) There came unto him a woman having an alabaster box of very precious ointment, and poured it on his head, as he sat at meat.

8) But when the disciples saw it, they had indignation, saying, to what purpose is this waste?

9) For this ointment might have been sold for much, and given to the poor.

10) When **Jesus** *understood it, he said unto them, why trouble ye the woman? For she hath wrought a good work upon me.*

11) For ye have the poor always with you; but ye have me not always.

12) For in that she hath poured this ointment on my body, she did it for my burial.

13) Verily I say unto you, Where-so-ever this gospel shall be preached in the whole world, there shall also this, that this woman hath done, be told for a memorial of her.

So now we understand that our **Lord and Master** says that a memorial is sometimes called for. But I want you to notice what the memorial is. **Jesus** tells his disciples to make a memorial of this woman's sacrifice! She poured her precious ointment on **his** head; to make **him** smell good on this most important religious holiday. The memorial is for her good deed, and not for herself. Notice that her name was not mentioned in these verses.

From that day until today there are children of **God** that continue to work good deeds, in the name of **Jesus**. And we want to leave them a memorial for their hard work. But we have to remember that the work that they accomplished was done by the grace of **God**. It was the **Holy Spirit** that actually did the deed, but it was the individual that opened their heart to the **Lord**.

So please admire the work done by the faithful, but remember that it was the **Lord** doing the work through the **Holy Spirit**.

MERCY AND TRUTH!

Mercy: Forgiveness or Kindness, particularly to a wrong-doer.

Truth: A proven sincerity, verity, honesty; righteousness.

(Proverbs 3: 3-6)

3) Let not mercy and truth forsake thee: bind them about thy neck; write them upon the table of thine heart:

4) So shalt thou find favour and good understanding in the sight of **GOD** *and man.*

5) Trust in the **LORD** *with all thine heart; and lean not unto thine own understanding.*

6) In all thy ways acknowledge him, and he shall direct thy Paths.

If **God** can forgive us for all of our sins, then we simply have no choice but to forgive others for their sins. If we truly want to be like our **Savior**, we must bind mercy and truth around our necks. Practice these day and night.

Let them become as familiar to us as breathing is. One day we will be in a place like no-other (**Heaven)!** There will be no room in our hearts for anything ungodly. Thank **God** for the ability to love one another!

MY CHILD'S NAME IS JESUS

(Matthew 1:18-21)

18) Now the birth of **Jesus Christ** *was on this wise: When as his mother Mary was espoused to Joseph, before they came together, she was found with child of the* **Holy Ghost**.

19) Then Joseph her husband, being a just man, and not willing to make her a publick example, was minded to put her away privily.

20) But while he thought on these things, behold, the **angel of the Lord** *appeared unto him in a dream, saying, "thou son of David, fear not to take unto thee Mary thy wife: for that which is conceived in her is of* **the Holy Ghost.**

21) And she shall bring forth a son, and thou shalt call his name **Jesus:** *for he shall save his people from their sins."*

I would like for you to pretend for just a moment. Pretend that it is you and your spouse that **God** decided to use to bring the savior into the world, instead of Joseph and Mary. How much more blessed do you think you would be than you are now? How much more would God do for you then? Why is it that The Bible does not speak a lot about the lives that Joseph and Mary had? Why are there not books or at least several chapters about them and their lives? They were the proud parents of **Jesus Christ!**

The reason is simple. They are not the saviors of the world, **Jesus Christ** is!

They are no closer to **God**, than you and I can be. The parents of **Jesus** are nothing to ignore for sure; but the point

I am trying to make is that life is all about the most precious gift that has ever been given to mankind. **It is all about Jesus! And not his parents, or us!**

NO CONDEMNATION!

1) There is now no condemnation to them which are in Christ Jesus, who walk not after the flesh, but after the Spirit.

(Romans 8:1)

When things get you down from everyday life, think of this verse and rejoice! Because you decided to accept Jesus as your Lord and Savior; you are no longer under the law, but are now under the grace of God! You cannot be condemned!

2) For the law of the Spirit of life in Christ Jesus hath made me free from the law of sin and death.

3) For what the law could not do, in that it was weak through the flesh, God sending his own son in the likeness of sinful flesh, and for sin, condemned sin in the flesh:

(Romans 8:2 and 3)

When Jesus died on the cross to clean us from our sin, and free us from being condemned; he in turn condemned sin to death. This does not mean that you can freely sin, but it does mean that if you confess your sin, it will be forgiven you.

But remember that God knows your heart, as well as your mind. So be sincere when you confess your sins, and try real hard not to sin again. Ask God to help you.

NO MORE TEARS

(Revelation 7:16 & 17)

16) They shall hunger no more; neither thirst any more, neither shall the sun light on them, nor any heat.

17) For **The Lamb** *which is in the midst of the throne shall feed them, and shall lead them unto living waters: and* **God shall wipe away all tears from their eyes.**

I can not speak for anyone else but me; but I plan on being one of those obedient children that **God** himself; wipes away my tears. Am I being greedy, wanting to be so close to **Jesus and God?** I believe smart is the word to use to describe my plans. And I want each one of you there with me! Do not forget that if you are a born again Christian, then you are one of **God's Children**. WOW! What a family! Thank you God! Thank you Jesus! Thank you Holy Spirit!

ONLE LANGUAGE!

God Makes Races and Creeds

(Genesis 11:1-9)

1) And the whole earth was of one language, and of one speech.

2) And it came to pass, as they journeyed from the east, that they found a plain in the land of Shi`nar; and they dwelt there.

3) And they said one to another, go to, let us make brick, and burn them thoroughly. And they had brick for stone, and slime had they for mortar.

4) And they said, go to, let us build us a city and a tower, whose top may reach unto heaven; and let us make a name, lest we be scattered abroad upon the face of the whole earth.

5) And the **Lord** *came down to see the city and the tower, which the children of men builded.*

6) And the **Lord** *said, behold, the people is one, and they have all one language; and this they begin to do: and now nothing will be restrained from them, which they have imagined to do.*

7) Go to, let us go down, and there **confound (confuse)** *their language, and they may not understand one another's speech.*

8) So the **Lord** *scattered them abroad from thence upon the face of all the earth: and they left off to build the city.*

*9) Therefore is the name of it called Babel; because the **Lord** did there confound the language of all the earth: and from thence did the **Lord** scatter them abroad upon the face of all the earth.*

God saw that all mankind was of the same race and language; and was spending their time trying to build one city; and a tower to reach heaven. This was not God's plan for mankind, to be in one place. He created an entire planet for man to enjoy and live. So he created different races; creeds; languages; and interests among his children. He wanted them to spread out among all the earth. Now we are all different, but yet we are still all ***God's*** children.

Now in our day and age, with the technology that we have, we know that the tower would have been a waste of time. The tower would have never reached heaven. We know that space is above earth, and there is no oxygen in space. Plus it would have had to have guide wires continuously.

We need to stay with Gods plan for us. And stop wasting our time on worldly things, which are destined to fail every time.

ONLY ONE GOD!

(Isaiah 43:12)

I have declared, and have saved, and I have shewed, when there was no strange God among you: therefore ye are my witnesses, saith the Lord, that I am your God.

(Isaiah 44:6)

Thus saith the Lord the king of Israel and his redeemer the Lord of hosts; I am the first, and I am the last; and beside me there is no God.

In these scriptures, God himself is reminding Israel that there is no other living God now or ever, but himself. He says that before he created this world and after this world is gone that he is and will always be the only God. He tells us that if we ask for forgiveness of our sins, that Jesus will forgive, and forget our sins.

If we believe that Jesus is the son of God; and that he died on the cross of Calvary to save us from our sins; then we become born again in our Spirit. We are now God's children, and not just his creation.

PASS ME THE SALT PLEASE!

Ye are the salt of the earth: but if the salt has lost his savour, wherewith shall it be salted? It is thenceforth good for nothing, but to be cast out, and to be trodden under foot of men. (Mathew 5: 13)

Jesus is talking about those who have received him as the Savior. We are then obligated to tell our lost brothers and sisters about him. Jesus is not only our savior, but also the flavor of our life, that is here on earth. If we seek him daily in our lives, then we can be guaranteed a better life now, full of the blessings that only he can give us. Plus his flavor never runs out, so we have no reason not to pass the salt - to everyone!!!

PATIENCE!

Have you prayed to God and asked him for a certain favor? Have you been asking for this favor for a long time? Does it seem like God did not hear you? Or maybe you asked when God was on vacation. Or maybe you think his answer is no, because it has not happened yet.

(Hebrews 10:36)

For ye have need of patience, that, after ye have done the will of God, ye might receive the promise.

One year is a long time to us. Five years is really a long time. But we have to remember that our Heavenly Father does not use our time to answer prayers. He does his will, in his time. I promise you that God is never on vacation when you call on him. And he hears and answers every prayer. Be longsuffering with your prayer, and trust God to answer. Learn Patience!

PRAYER; HOW DO WE PRAY?

(Romans 8:26 and 27)

26) Likewise the Spirit also helpeth our infirmities: for we know not what we should pray for as we ought: but the Spirit itself maketh intercession for us with groanings which cannot be uttered.

27) And he that searcheth the hearts knoweth what is in the mind of the Spirit, because he maketh intercession for saints according to the will of God.

If are are a Christian (a believer of Christ) and are saved, then the Holy Spirit is living inside you. And he is the one who makes intercession on your behalf. You cannot be in the presence of our Almighty God because of the sin that you have in your flesh; but the Holy Spirit can, and does for you.

So when you pray remember that the Holy Spirit will relay your wants to Jesus, and if you cannot think of the best way to ask; do not worry. The Holy Spirit knows exactly what to say and how to say it.

REWARD'S COME WITH OBEDIENCE!

(Deuteronomy 5:29)

O that there were such an heart in them, that they would fear me, and keep all my commandments always, that it might be **well with them**, *and with their children forever!*

No matter where in the Bible you read, and study; you see that **God** loves us and demands that we are faithful to follow his commandments.

But he also rewards those who are obedient. In a world where most of **Gods** children only obey sometimes; the rewards are scarce and often unnoticed! **God** loves us all so much! That he really wants to reward us, but we are going to have to be obedient to him to receive our rewards!

Let's do our part for him; not for the rewards; but for our love for him, and his son, and his spirit. And let **Gods** rewards flow on us in our lives as **God** intended. And always be thankful to **God** when he gives you rewards. May **God bless you and your family**?

WHAT REWARD'S DO I RECEIVE FOR BECOMING ONE OF GOD'S CHILDREN?

(Ezekiel 36:25-30)

25) Then will I sprinkle clean water upon you, and ye shall be clean; from all your filthiness, and from all your idols, will I cleanse you.

26) A new heart also will I give you, and a new spirit will I put within you: and I will take away the stoney heart out of your flesh, and I will give you an heart of flesh.

27) And I will put my spirit within you, and cause you to walk in my statutes, and ye shall keep my judgments, and do them.

28) And ye shall dwell in the land that I gave to your fathers; and ye shall be my people, and I will be your God.

29) I will also save you from all your uncleanliness: and I will call for the corn, and will increase it, and lay no famine upon you.

30) And I will multiply the fruit of the tree, and the increase of the field, that ye shall receive no more reproach of famine among the heathen.

God told Ezekiel to tell the land of Israel, that if they would repent, and turn from their evil ways, and be his people; that he would give them that which he had promised to their fathers. Now we all know that the children of Israel are God's chosen children; so how do we as American's get in on this promise from God?

Later in the New Testament we find out that God sends his only begotten son (Jesus). That who so-ever believes in him, will not only (not) die; but also become a new creation. A child of God! One of his chosen people! Bingo! We are in with the promise!

If you could understand how much God loves you, and wants you for his own; you would gladly be obedient to his statutes and testaments. In return he gives you absolutely everything he promised his other children (the Israelites).

Thank you for loving us father! I do accept your precious son Jesus as my Savior. And I will gladly be one of your children. Thank you God!

THE SECOND COMMANDMENT

(Exodus 20:4)

Thou shalt not make unto thee any graven image, or any likeness of any thing that is in heaven above, or that is in the earth beneath, or that is in the water under the earth."

The definition of a graven image is an object of worship carved usually from wood or stone. Now we all have images in our life; so we are not being obedient to our father's word. You can argue with me all day; but that is not going to change Gods word! I too have failed him in this commandment. I do not have a graven image anywhere, but I do have likenesses of myself, wife, children, family, friends, Jesus, flowers, wildlife etc...

What I am doing is making sure that I do not worship any of my likenesses except one of them (Jesus). I Love all the rest of them. I thank God for everything in my life.

God wants, and deserves all our worship and love. And in return for our obedience, he is willing to give us everything in his kingdom. He even gave us his only begotten son Jesus; to show us the way home one day.

Pray and talk to God yourself about the images in your life, and make sure he is the only one that you worship. And worship Jesus; because when you worship Jesus; you are worshiping God! And always be thankful to God for everything.

SIN SHALL STOP!

(Romans 5:21)

That as sin hath reigned unto death, even so might grace reign through righteousness unto eternal life by Jesus Christ our Lord.

Here we see that sin will leave our lives at our death. And that grace might reign for eternity through Jesus Christ. Paul says that grace might reign, because to receive grace you must be a born again Christian. And not everyone will receive Jesus as their sacrifice for sin. Therefore their sin has not been forgiven, and they will answer for all their own sin. Everything they have ever done in their entire life!

But the ones who have accepted their Savior Jesus, and have confessed and asked for forgiveness, their sins are no more. And Jesus will not bring them up to you on judgment day.

Have you been saved and forgiven? Or are you willing to answer for every sin that you have ever committed?

STAY FOCUSED!

(Mark 1:36 thru 38)

36) And Simon and they that were with him followed after him.

37) And when they had found him, they said unto him, all men seek for thee.

38) And he said unto them; ***Let us go into the next towns that I may preach there also: for therefore came I forth.***

In the verses before these, we read that Jesus has been healing those that are diseased, and casting out many devils (verse 34). And early, before the rising of the sun, Jesus went to a solitary place and was praying to God (verse 35).

Simon and the others found him, and let him know that a lot of men were asking for him, for healing no doubt! Jesus told them that they were leaving for the next town, so he could continue preaching.

Jesus reminded them that he did not come for the healing of the body. He came to tell them how to be saved for all eternity. His healing was for ever and ever. Jesus never got side-tracked from his purpose, to preach. Even though there were a lot of distractions going on around him, he stayed focused!

We also need to be focused on what our mighty Savior has set for us to do. We also have a lot of interruptions in our life, but we can still stay focused!

TEMPTATION!

We are <u>all</u> under the attack of Temptation! Our precious Savior was even tempted by Satan himself. Of course Jesus did not fall to temptation, but we are not as strong as he.

So how do we as children of God fight this stuff that seems to come at us from all sides?

(Galatians 5:16 & 17)

16) This I say then, Walk in the **Spirit**, *and ye shall not fulfill the lust of the flesh.*

17) For the flesh lusteth against the **Spirit**, *and the* **Spirit** *against the flesh: and these are contrary the one to the other; so that ye cannot do the things that ye would.*

Paul understood that all of us are tempted. We cannot stop the temptation itself; but we can use it to our own advantage! If we call on Jesus every time we are under attack, instead of trying to fight it on our own; then we will find out that we are getting closer to our Savior, and not farther away.

THE TENTH COMMANDMENT

(Exodus 20:17)

17) Thou shalt not covet thy neighbor's house; thou shalt not covet thy neighbor's wife, nor his manservant, nor his maidservant, nor his ox, nor his ass, nor anything that is thy neighbor's

(Luke 12: 13-15)

13) And one of the company said unto him, Master, speak to my brother, that he divide the inheritance with me.

14) And he said unto him, Man, who made me a judge or a divider over you?

15)_And he said unto them, Take heed, and beware of covetousness: for a man's life consisteth not in the abundance of the things which he possesseth.

Jesus tells the crowd to be very careful not to put any interest into possessions. And do not be jealous of any other ones possessions. Then he tells them a parable.

(Luke 12: 16 thru 21)

16) And he spake a parable unto them, saying, the ground of a certain rich man brought forth plentifully:

17) And he thought within himself, saying, what shall I do, because I have no room where to bestow my fruits?

18) And he said, this will I do: I will pull down my barns, and build greater; and there will I bestow all my fruits and my goods.

19) And I will say to my soul, Soul, thou hast much goods laid up for many years; take thine ease, eat, drink, and be merry.

20) But **God** *said unto him,* ***Thou fool****, this night thy soul shall be required of thee: then whose shall those things be, which thou hast provided?*

21) So is he that layeth up treasure for himself, and is not rich toward **God***.*

Take this message to heart! **God** will call you a <u>fool</u> if you spend your life trying to gain possessions of the world for yourself and your family. You can not serve two masters!

Some preachers will lead you to believe that your possessions are blessings from **God**; but if you read your Bible you will know that anything extra is to be given to the poor.

(Luke 12: 6 and 7)

6) Are not five sparrows sold for two farthings, and not one of them is forgotten before God?

7) But even the very hairs of your head are all numbered. Fear not therefore: ye are of more value than many sparrows.

Jesus is telling the multitude there that day, and he is telling us the same thing today that God loves us more than anything he has created. He also wants us to trust in **<u>him</u>** for our needs. The treasures of this world are only temporary, but the treasures of God are going to last us forever!

Spend your time learning to be obedient to your Savior **Jesus**, and getting closer to him!

Your rewards will be great in heaven if you stay focused on Jesus!

And do not wish you had anything that someone else has; for if God wanted you to have those things, then you would have them! He wants you to have eternal life in his kingdom.

THE BEGINNING OF TIME!

(Genesis 1:1-5)

1) In the beginning **God** *created the heaven and the earth.*

2) And the earth was without form, and void; and darkness was upon the face of the deep. And the **Spirit of God** *moved upon the face of the waters.*

3) And **God** *said, "Let there be light": and there was light.*

4) And **God** *saw the light, that it was good: and* **God** *divided the light from the darkness.*

5) And **God** *called the light day, and the darkness* **he** *called night. And the evening and the morning were the first day.*

In the first day **God** created a planet and a Light. But he also created a measurement of time that **he** called a day! The darkness was already here.

(Genesis 1:6-8)

6) And **God** *said, "Let there be a firmament in the midst of the waters, and let it divide the waters from the waters."*

7) And **God** *made the firmament, and divided the waters which were under the firmament from the waters which were above the firmament: and it was so.*

8) And **God** *called the firmament heaven. And the evening and the morning were the second day.*

God has now created the firmament (sky).

(Genesis 1:9-13)

9) And **God** *said, Let the waters under the heaven be gathered together unto one place, and let the dry land appear: and it was so.*

10) And **God** *called the dry land earth; and the gathering together of the waters called* **he** *seas: and* **God** *saw that it was good.*

11) And **God** *said, "Let the earth bring forth grass, the herb yielding seed, and the fruit tree yielding fruit after his kind, whose seed is in itself, upon the earth": and it was so.*

12) And the earth brought forth grass and herb yielding seed after his kind, and the tree yielding fruit, whose seed was within itself, after his kind: and **God** *saw that it was good.*

13) And the evening and the morning were the third day.

Now in only three of **God's** days we have a sun, a planet with an atmosphere, a measurement of time, seas and land, grasses and trees with fruit, and seeds to continue the grasses and trees with fruit.

(Genesis 1:14-19)

14) And **God** *said, let there be lights in the firmament of the heaven to divide the day from the night; and let them be for signs, and for seasons, and for days, and years:*

15) And let them be for lights in the firmament of the heaven to give light upon the earth: and it was so.

16) And **God** *made two great lights; the greater light to rule the day, and the lesser light to rule the night:* **he** *made the stars also.*

17) And **God** *set them in the firmament of the heaven to give light upon the earth,*

18) And to rule over the day and over the night, and to divide the light from the darkness: and **God** *saw that it was good.*

19) And the evening and the morning were the fourth day.

Now **God** has expanded our time for months and years. **He** has also created a moon so the darkness will not be overwhelming. And **he** hung stars all over the atmosphere.

(Genesis 1: 20-23)

20) And **God** *said, let the waters bring forth abundantly the moving creature that hath life, and fowl that may fly above the earth in the open firmament of heaven.*

21) And **God** *created great whales, and every living creature that moveth, which the waters brought forth abundantly, after their kind, and every winged fowl after his kind: and* **God** *saw that it was good.*

22) And **God** *blessed them, saying, Be fruitful and multiply, and fill the waters in the seas, and let the fowl multiply in the earth.*

23) And the evening and the morning were the fifth day.

God has now filled the waters and the sky with life. And commanded them all to multiply.

(Genesis 1: 24-31)

24) And **God** *said, Let the earth bring forth the living creature after his kind, cattle, and creeping thing, and beast of the earth after his kind: and it was so.*

25) And **God** *made the beast of the earth after his kind, and cattle after their kind, and every thing that creepeth upon the earth after his kind: and* **God** *saw that it was good.*

26) And **God** *said, Let us make man in our image, after our likeness: and let them have have dominion over the fish of the sea, and over the fowl of the air, and over the cattle, and over all the earth, and over every creeping thing that creepeth upon the earth.*

27) So **God** *created man in* **his** *own image, in the image of* **God** *created* **he** *him; male and female created* **he** *them.*

28) And **God** *blessed them, and* **God** *said unto them, be fruitful, and multiply, and replenish the earth, and subdue it: and have dominion over the fish of the sea, and over the fowl of the air, and over every living thing that moveth upon the earth.*

29) And **God** *said, Behold, I have given you every herb bearing seed, which is upon the face of all the earth, and every tree, in the which is the fruit of a tree yielding seed; to you it shall be for meat.*

30) And to every beast of the earth, and to every fowl of the air, and to every thing that creepeth upon the earth, wherein there is life, **I** *have given every green herb for meat: and it was so.*

31) And **God** *saw every thing that* **he had made**, *and, behold, it was very good. And the evening and the morning were the sixth day.*

In only six of **God's** days **he** has now completed the world as we know it! **He** has created every living thing on the earth, and also man and woman to take care of it! **He** gave us dominion over every thing on this planet! Now I can not tell you what to believe about how the world got here! I can only tell you the truth! Believe what your heart tells you to believe. But for me; I am staying with **God!**

THE BIBLE IS THE WORD OF GOD!

(John 1:1)

In the beginning was the word, and the word was with GOD, And the word was GOD.

(Revelation 22:7)

Behold, I come quickly; blessed is he that keepeth the sayings of the prophecy of this book.

Is it okay to read other religious books besides The Holy Bible? It depends on the book! Always cross reference the book you want to read with The Holy Bible. If there is a difference to the other book, then throw that book away. The Holy Bible is the only word of God. All other books are either a translation of Gods word, or a testimony. Testimonies are great because they tell what God has done for someone, or explains how God has worked in someone's life. We always need to give our father in heaven Praise and Glory. But we need to know The Holy Bible, so that we can tell if another book is true or not. Remember that there is only one book that tells the word of God. And his word is all we need for anything we might face in life.

THE BIG BANG THEORY

(John 1:1 thru 10)

1) In the beginning was the word, and the word was with **God**, *and the word was* **God.**

2) The same was in the beginning with **God**.

3) All things were made by him; and without him was not any thing made that was made.

4) In him was life (Jesus); and the life was the light of men.

5) And the light shineth in darkness; and the darkness comprehended it not.

6) There was a man sent from **God**, *whose name was John.*

7) The same came for a witness, to bear witness of the light that all men through him might believe.

8) He was not the light, but was sent to bear witness of that light.

9) That was the true light, which lighteth every man that cometh into the world.

10) He was in the world, and the world was made by him, and the world knew him not.

You read it for yourself in The Holy Bible. It simply says that there was absolutely nothing, before **God** himself made it! It says nothing about a big bang, or any other kind of noise! If a bunch of atoms had bumped into each other, and formed this Universe; then that would have been it! Then as soon as they joined together, then they would have started to become abnormal, and shaped themselves differently. The Universe would have started to come apart. I have heard the theory of Evolution. And if we were first Apes, then all apes would be men. If you believe these theories (lies), then you must be walking in a daze! None of this makes any sense at all!

But the Bible tells of an almighty **God** that made everything we can see, and even the things that we cannot see. An Almighty **God** that not only made us, but loves us more than anything else that **he** made! **He** gave the believers an eternal life with him in his kingdom through his only begotten son **Jesus**.

I cannot tell you what to believe, but I can tell you to open your eyes, and see this beautiful world **God** has made for you! And then I can tell you to call on **God's** only son **Jesus**; and **he** will show you a heaven that is even more beautiful!

THE GREATEST VICTORY OF ALL TIME

When Adam and Eve did eat the fruit of the tree of knowledge of good and evil; mankind was condemned to die. Satan had defeated ***Gods*** creation, man.

(John 3:16)

*For **God** so loved the world, that he gave his only begotten son. That whosoever believeth in him should not perish, but have everlasting life.*

For mankind to live, ***Jesus*** must die, and defeat our sins. So ***Jesus*** was born into the world, to tell of his loving father, who loves us all. He first shows us the way of how we as children of ***God*** (Through Him), can be saved from death. (***Gods*** son defeats Satan).

*So **Jesus** dies on the cross to save mankind from his sins. Now when we die, we can die without sin (If we ask **Jesus** to forgive us). But we still must die, and that's the end.*

*But **God** had a better plan. **Jesus** was not only to die for our sins; but also be raised from the dead after 3 days. Those who believe that **Jesus** was raised from the grave and have accepted him as their Savior; will also be raised from the grave. **God** has now defeated Satan in life.*

(Matthew 16:21)

From that time forth began **Jesus** *to shew unto his disciples, how that he must go unto Jerusalem, and suffer many things of the elders and chief priests and scribes, and be killed, and be raised again the third day. This is the greatest victory of all time!*

THE LAW SHALL STAND!

(Matthew 1:17&18)

Think not that I am come to destroy the law, or the prophets: I am not come to destroy, but to fulfill. For verily I say unto you, till heaven and earth pass, one jot or one tittle shall in no wise pass from the law, till all be fulfilled.

Jesus, our Lord and Master spoke these words in a sermon to let all those who think the laws that God gave to Moses, are no longer in effect. He says strongly that those laws will be our laws, until the end of time.

This is where Denominations originated from. Some religions believe the word of God means this, while others believe it means something else. What should you do to find out what Gods words mean to you and your family? First pray and ask God to give you understanding of his word; and then diligently seek him, in his word. He has given us The Bible for a reason.

THE LORD IS GOOD!

(Nahum 1:7)

The Lord Is Good, a strong hold in the day of trouble; and he knoweth them that trust in him.

When **Jesus** (The King of Kings, and the only begotten **Son Of God**) was born; was he born into the world in the largest Castle? No! Was he born into the richest family? No! Was he born in a time of great peace? No!

When the greatest gift to mankind was born, there was terrific trouble for the family he was to be born into. Joseph and Mary were on the run for **Jesus'** life! He was placed in a manger (a troft where food for animals was placed) after his birth, and not in a soft baby bed. He was born into a troubled world on purpose! To show us that he understands our trouble, and will help-if we trust him!

THE TEN COMMANDMENTS

(Exodus 20: 3-17)

1) Thou shalt have no other God's before me.

2) Thou shalt not make unto thee any graven image, or any likeness of anything that is in Heaven above, or that is in the earth beneath, or that is in the water under the earth.

3) Thou shalt not take the name of the Lord thy God in vain.

4) Remember the sabbath day, to keep it Holy!

5) Honour thy Father and thy Mother.

6) Thou shalt not kill.

7) Thou shalt not commit adultery.

8) Thou shalt not steal.

9) Thou shalt not bear false witness against thy neighbor.

10) Thou shalt not covet thy neighbors house, thou shalt not covet thy neighbors wife, nor his manservant, nor his maid servant, nor his ox, nor his ass, nor anything that is thy neighbors.

The Ten Commandments are from God! Not a prophet, or an apostle, or a preacher. The creator of all things gave Moses these laws; for all mankind! No, the laws will not get you into Heaven, only Jesus can. But these laws must be obeyed. If you want God to be there for you; then you must be obedient to him, and his word. He is not going to bless disobedience! Instead, he will punish disobedience.

Learn his laws and statues, and remember them. Share them with your children and grandchildren. And most of all, place these laws into your life, and obey them daily!

Follow the way Jesus lived, and you will never have to worry about sinning against God.

THE TESTIMONY OF A SINNER!

I was born the fourth child in a family of five, in the year 1956, in the month of June. I was named by two great aunts that I have no memory of. They were Christians for sure because they named me after two of Jesus' disciples (James and Andrew).

I remember going to church often. My father was a Deacon and a Sunday school teacher. My mother was also a Sunday school teacher, and the piano, and organ player. I also remember singing in front of the congregation a song, "You got to say no to the Devil Everyday".

We were considered a middle class family, with a descent three bedroom house in a nice neighborhood. We had our friends and family, and were very happy for awhile. Then, when I was 10 years old Satan showed his ugly face at the Feathers residence.

My mother's best friend, who came over every morning for coffee; and my father decided to run away together. They both had taken their eyes off Jesus, and affixed them on each other. My father left 5 children, and she left 4 of her own. The worse part is that they would not support their children. They forgot their children just like they forgot Jesus.

So after mom sold the house, we moved to California. We lived there for about 6 months, and then moved back to Florida to live with one of my aunts. I remember in one year, going to three different high schools. I do not remember going to church anymore, I guess mom blamed God for what happened. My mother passed away when I was 29 years old. By then, I had been married and divorced, with two daughters.

I am moving quickly through this period of my life because I was really messed up in my mind and heart. I was an alcoholic and a user of drugs. I was a very selfish person who only cared for me. I really thought I was good looking, and that all the women wanted to be with me.

I remember being baptized when I was 9 or 10 years old, but I was born again many years later. I had turned my back on Jesus too, but he never turned his back on me.

When I remarried three years after my divorce, I thought I was ready to grow up; but I was wrong. I was still under the control of Satan. I still drank everyday with my buddies. But when I reached the age of 43, God had seen enough! I got sick one hot afternoon, and after days of getting worse, I went to the doctor. The Doctor diagnosed me with Rheumatoid Arthritis. He referred me to a Rheumatologist, who after several weeks referred me to a Hematologist (Blood Specialist).

The Hematologist was also an Oncologist (Cancer Specialist). After several blood tests, the Doctor told my wife and me that I had Leukemia. She was certain that I had Leukemia, but that there were different kinds, and she would have to take more tests to determine which kind. You might be thinking, well good, could not have happened to a worse man! I personally in my heart had given up on living a long time. One afternoon while I was walking in my front yard, and feeling sorry for myself, God revealed to me the man I had become. I fell to my knees and prayed. I asked God to forgive me for all my sins, and made a covenant with him right there. I promised him that what ever I had left (days) to live, that I wanted him to use me anyway <u>he</u> saw fit. He told me that he accepted my promise, but that it was going to be him and me, and that my family would not be supporting my decision. But when I got to the place in my walk with him, where he wanted me to be, he would bring my family to me.

Now you might be thinking, "Why would God use such a man?" A man that abused peoples feelings for his own self satisfaction. Because he is God! He is the only one who can change a person completely! Just like he said, "You must be born again."

After more blood work, and then a bone marrow test, the doctor was ready to reveal what I had. I remember sitting on the edge of the bed waiting for her to reveal which disease I had. After several minutes she looked at us with a confused expression, and said "I do not know what you have, but it is not cancer."

After six weeks of tests, I returned to work. Two weeks after going back to work, I had a Heart Attack. I had a blocked artery, and had a stint placed inside the artery to prevent it from closing up again. Many changes have occurred in me, but that is a longer version of this testimony. God cured me from smoking cigarettes, a bad habit that I fought with for thirty one years. Of course Drugs and Alcohol are also a thing of the past.

Now it has been 6 years since I was reborn, and I have been gifted with the understanding of the word of God. He says he will reveal his word to babes; and I am surely his baby! A child of God thanks to the sacrifice of my brother Jesus!

If God can use me for his glory, then I promise you he can use you also. If you want to change your life and want God to receive you as one of his own, then you too must confess your sins, and ask for forgiveness. And let him use you for his glory, and you will be amazed at what he will do.

This Testimony is still on going, and I cannot wait to see what he is going to do next. I have read the new testament three times and the entire Bible once. It is the most fantastic book that has ever been published. I know it to be the word of God, and everything within it is the truth.

Read it for yourself, with Gods help of course! He will reveal his word to you too.

I have never felt better inside in my entire life! God has truly forgiven my sins, and he has not forgotten the covenant between him and me; and neither have I. I wait for his next order!

THE THIRD COMMANDMENT

(Be Very Careful What You Say!)

I hear God's name in vain spoken quite often, at work, in public, and even at relative's houses. What does God say about this situation?

(Exodus 20:7)

"Thou shalt not take the name of the Lord thy God in vain: for the Lord will not hold him guiltless that taketh his name in vain."

That word is coming from God himself! Besides getting God's anger directed towards you, which should be more fear then that is needed to get the point across; think about how you would feel if this was done to you.

What if I called out your name, and got your attention; and then I ignored you.

What if I did that over and over several times? Would you get angry with me? If you did that to me, not only would I get angry with you; but I would eventually ignore you.

When you say God's name, and get an almighty God's attention; you better be in the right mind and spirit to speak to him! I do not believe that you want God to ignore you, so do not attempt to abuse his name! You will answer for it!

So when you hear someone saying God's name in vain next time; remind them in private, what danger that person is putting their self into. Remind them what one of the Ten Commandments are, and suggest that they learn the other nine.

TRIAL'S AND TRIBULATION'S; WHAT GOOD ARE THEY?

Why do we have trials and tribulations Father? They only make us mad, sad, or worried, don't they?

(Romans 5:1-5)

1) Therefore being justified by faith, we have peace with God through our Lord Jesus Christ:

2) By whom also we have access by faith into this grace wherein we stand, and rejoice in hope of the glory of God.

3) And not only so, but we glory in tribulation also: knowing that tribulation worketh patience;

4) And patience, experience; and experience, hope:

5) And hope maketh not ashamed; because the love of God is shed abroad in our hearts by the Holy Ghost which is given unto us.

Wow! There is a lot of good that I can receive with my troubles. I do want patience, experience, peace with God, and hope in my future.

I didn't realize how much good could come of trials and tribulations. I also see that when we go through bad situations, that we grow in faith; because we call on Jesus for help.

And we do gain experience about that particular problem. Now we can give comfort and advice to someone else who is going through the same thing.

I do not know what trial is awaiting me next. But I do know that my Savior is with me, and will give me something good after I get through it.

Thank You Jesus for my trials and tribulations! I thank you for your love and help. Glory is to you Master!

WEAPONS ARE USELESS!

(Isaiah 54:17)

No weapon that is formed against thee shall prosper; and every tongue that shall rise against thee in judgment thou shalt condemn. This is the heritage of the servants of the Lord, and their righteousness is of me, saith the Lord.

Understand that serving and worshiping are different. You do them at the same time when you serve *God*!

But you can worship *God* without serving him. Be warned that if you decide to serve *God* that Satan will come after you. But *God* says that no weapon that is formed against you will succeed. And that anyone that is against you shall not prosper in their efforts. Righteousness is a gift from *God* to his children who have accepted his son *Jesus* as their savior. And *God* loves his children and would not let anything bad happen to them. So serve *God* without fear of evil, knowing that *Jesus* is with you at all times.

WHAT CAN ONE MAN DO?

(Romans 5:12)

Wherefore, as by one man sin entered into the world, and death by sin; and so death passed upon all men, for that all have sinned.

One man brought us sin in our lives. His name is Adam. And because of his disobedience to God, death also was brought upon all men.

(Romans 5:15)

But not as the offence, so also is the free gift. For if through the offence of one many be dead, much more the grace of God, and the gift by grace, which is by one man, Jesus Christ, hath abounded unto many.

And now thanks are to our Lord and Savior Jesus (one man); we do not have to stay dead! Because of the grace of God and the love of Jesus; many of us will live for ever!

Do you see how much one man, or woman, can affect all of us? Be careful of what you say or do, because our almighty God has very good ears and eyes. But praise is to the same God, that he is willing to forgive us of our sins, if we will only confess them to him and ask for that forgiveness!

WHAT SINS, I DO NOT REMEMBER THEM!

(Isaiah 43:25)

I, even I, am he that blotted out thy transgressions for mine own sake, and will not remember your sins.

God told Isaiah that it is he that can eliminate or forgive his transgressions. And he tells Isaiah that he will not remember them. Praise **God!** We were born into a sinful world, and in a sinful body. But we can be forgiven for all of our sins, and not have to answer for them. That is of course if we except **Jesus** as our Savior, and ask him to forgive us.

Sins are not automatically cleansed on their own. We must first confess them to our **Lord**, and then try our very best not to continue in our sin. **Thank you Jesus for loving us!**

WHAT WOULD YOU GIVE?

How much would you give for a home in the richest neighborhood in the land? What about in the entire universe?

There is a mansion in Heaven that is available for you. Not only will you have God, Jesus, and the Holy Spirit as neighbors; but also those other rich relatives that went on to glory-land ahead of you.

It's a home that will never need repairs. You will never have to paint it. You will never have to have it pressure washed. You will never have to cut your lawn, or prune your flowers and trees. Best of all, this Mansion has already been paid for! Jesus bought your mansion with his blood! Don't you want to at least get to know this man who gave <u>his</u> life to save <u>yours</u>? Can you give him praise? Can you give him prayer? Can you give him thanks? Where were you on Sunday?

WHERE IS THE KINGDOM OF GOD?

(Luke 17: 20-21)

20) And when he was demanded of the Pharisee's, when the kingdom of God should come, he answered them and said, The kingdom of God cometh not with observation:

21) Neither shall they say, Lo here! Or lo there! For behold, the kingdom of God is within you!

I have heard a lot of people say that certain churches are dead. The Holy Spirit wasn't there when they attended. The preacher was not very good, or the sermon did not do anything for them.

Every church that I have attended, the Holy Spirit was there! And I went to the same churches that they attended! The difference is that when the church was empty with people, then the Holy Spirit really wasn't there! The Holy Spirit and the kingdom of God do not reside in buildings! They are found in those who are born again Christians. When I go to the store for gas or bread, the Holy Spirit is there. When I go to work, the kingdom of God is there! Everywhere I go the Holy Spirit, and the kingdom of God is there! I know this because they reside in me, and I take them everywhere!

Are they everywhere you are? Or are you still looking for them?

WHERE IS YOUR CROSS?

(Matthew 10:38)

Jesus said And he that taketh not his cross, and followeth after me, is not worthy of me.

Jesus meant that if you do not follow his lead, then you are not worthy of being called one of his followers. He not only told us how we are to live our lives, but he walked the earth for many years and showed us how to live.

Our cross is our soul. We cannot serve two masters. We have to choose to follow Jesus, or the things of man. You cannot take up your cross and leave it too. So where are you going to place your cross?

WHERE WAS GOD?

(Acts 27:18-26)

18) And we being exceedingly tossed with a tempest, the next day they lightened the ship;

Tempest: A violent wind, usually attended with rain, snow, or hail.

19) And the third day we cast out with our own hands the tackling of the ship.

Tackling: To change ones direction on a ship. To navigate.

20) And when neither sun nor stars in many days appeared, and no small tempest lay on us, all hope that we should be saved was then taken away.

Here is Paul and a company of soldiers on a ship. When you read chapter 27 and 28, you see that Paul is being taken to appear before Caesar, to be judged.

The ship that they are traveling on is in great danger. You might ask where God is.

21) But after long abstinence Paul stood forth in the midst of them, and said, Sirs, ye should have hearkened unto me, and now have loosed from Crete, and to have gained this harm and loss.

22) And now I exhort you to be of good cheer: for there shall be no loss of any man's life among you, but of the ship.

Paul has prophesized to the men on the ship that they will survive, but that the ship will not. Where is God now?

23) For there stood by me this night the angel of God, whose I am, and whom I serve,

24) Saying, Fear not, Paul; thou must be brought before Caesar; and lo, God hath given thee all them that sail with thee.

25) Wherefore, sirs, be of good cheer: for I believe God, that it shall be even as it was told me.

26) Howbeit we must be cast upon a certain island.

Now we know that Paul and company were not the only ones on the ship through the terrible storm. God was there! And all there troubles are not yet over. They are to be shipwrecked on a certain island. Paul is going to be bitten by a venomous viper.

(Acts 28:3-5)

3) And when Paul had gathered a bundle of sticks, and laid them on the fire, there came a viper out of the heat, and fastened on his hand.

4) And when the Barbarians saw the venomous beast hang on his hand, they said among themselves, No doubt this man is a murderer, whom, though he had escaped the sea, yet vengeance suffereth not to live.

5) And he shook off the beast into the fire, and felt no harm.

Now that they have escaped the sinking ship and made it to shore; you can plainly see that Paul's problems are not over yet. Where was God? The same place he has always been; right there in the middle of everything, with Paul! God never said that any of us would not face all kinds of trials and tribulations.

But if you are his child, then he will be there with you every time. And will help you through the problems, just as he was with Paul. So do not get too caught up in your trials and tribulations to call on the only one who can help you. He loves you so much, and wants you to be victorious in everything.

REMEMBER WHERE YOU CAME FROM!

(*God* creates the heaven and the earth)

In the beginning God created the Heaven and the earth. And the earth was without form, and void; and darkness was upon the face of the deep. And the Spirit of God moved upon the face of the waters. (Genesis 1:1 and 2)

(*God* creates man and woman)

So God created man in his own image, in the image of God created he him; male and female created he them. And God blessed them, and God said unto them; be fruitful, and multiply, and replenish the earth. And subdue it: and have dominion over the fish of the sea, and over the fowl of the air, and over every living creature that moveth upon the earth. (Genesis 1:27 and 28)

(Man and Woman sin by disobeying *God*)

And the Lord God commanded the man saying, of every tree of the garden thou mayest freely eat; but of the tree of the knowledge of good and evil, thou shalt not eat of it: for in the day that thou eatest thereof thou shalt surely die. (Genesis 2:16 and 17)

And the serpent said unto the woman, ye shall not surely die: for God doth know that in the day ye eat thereof, then your eyes shall be opened, and ye shall be as gods; knowing good and evil."And when the woman saw that the tree was good for food, and that it was pleasant to the eyes, and a tree to be desired to make one wise, she took of the fruit thereof; and did eat, and gave also unto her husband with her; and he did eat. And the eyes of them both were opened, and they knew that they were naked: and they sewed fig leaves together, and made themselves aprons. (Genesis 3:4 thru 7)

(God sends his only begotten son to save mankind)

And so it was that while they were there, the days were accomplished that she should be delivered. And she brought forth her firstborn son, and wrapped him in swaddling clothes, and laid him in a manger: because there was no room in the inn. (Luke 2: 6 and 7)

(Jesus must die for our sins)

Saying, The son of man must be delivered into the hands of sinful men, and be cruicified, and the third day rise again. (Luke 24:7)

Jesus answered and said unto him: Verily, verily, I say unto thee; except a man be born again he cannot see the kingdom of God. Nicode`mus saith unto him; How can a man be born when he is old? Can he enter, the second time into his mothers womb and be born? Jesus answered, Verily, verily, I say unto thee. Except a man be born of water and of the Spirit, he cannot enter into the kingdom of God. (John 3:3 thru 5)

That whosoever believeth in him should not perish, but have eternal life. For God so loved the world, that he gave his only begotten son, that whosoever believeth in him, shall not perish, but will have everlasting life. (John 3:15 and 16)

We must freely accept *Jesus* as the son of *God*, and as our savior from sins with all of our heart, our soul, our mind, and all our strength.

WHO IS YOUR FATHER?

(John 8:43-47)

43) Why do ye not understand my speech? Even because ye cannot hear my word.

44) Ye are of your father the devil, and the lusts of your father ye will do! He was a murderer from the beginning; and abode not in the truth, because there is no truth in him. When he speaketh a lie, he speaketh of his own: for he is a liar, and a father of it.

45) And because I tell you the truth, ye believe me not.

46) Which of you convinceth me of sin? And if I say the truth, why do ye not believe me?

47) He that is of **God** *heareth* **God's words***: ye therefore hear them not, because ye are* **not of God**.

Now I will ask you again; who is your Father? Do you hear the words of **God**? Or are you listening to the Devil? You might say that, that is a stupid question; but your answer may surprise even you!

You do not even have to answer **Jesus**, because he already knows. But I am of the flesh, and can only tell who your father is, by the way that you live.

If you are consumed in the things of the world; then you are a child of Satan! And if you are consumed in **God's** word, and the teachings therein, then you are a child of **God**. You might then say I do some of the things of **God**, and some of the things of **Satan**; now who is my father?

If you are a child of Satan, then you will not care about your sins. But if you are a child of **God**, then you will be miserable in your life until you ask your father to forgive you of those sins, and you will try your best not to do them again!

The question may not even matter to you right now; but it soon will! Which one does your life represent?

Do you worship **Jesus** or the things of this world (Satan)? Do you read the Bible to see what your father wants you to do? Or do you just read books written by man? Do you watch what you say? Or just watch to see what everyone else is doing?

WHO SAY'S THAT I AM POOR; YOU?

(James 2:5)

Hearken, my beloved brethren. Hath not **God** *chosen the poor of this world rich in faith, and heirs of the kingdom which he hath promised to them that love him.*

James is warning his brethren to stop despising the poor of this world.

(James 2:4)

Are ye not then partial in yourselves, and are become judges of evil thoughts.

He reminds them that **God** chooses the poor far more often than the rich to do his good work. The rich are not responsible enough to handle such important work, because they are always trying to see something in it for themselves! Yes, there are a few chosen in the Bible that were wealthy, but they were strong enough in faith to handle the wealth. And they used their wealth for the glory of **God**; not themselves!

(Mark 6:7 thru 9)

And he called unto him the twelve, and began to send them forth by two and two; and gave them power over unclean spirits; And commanded them that they should take nothing for their journey, save a staff only; no script, no bread, no money in their purse: But be shod with sandals; and not put on two coats.

Why do you think **Jesus** would send his disciples out into the world, and tell them not to take anything with them but a staff only? What are they going to eat? Where will they sleep? How will they survive? Where will they go?

Now they are really in a fix. They are poor, and in the cruel world with nothing to eat and nowhere to sleep. They do not even know where they are going.

Jesus knows how they will survive! He will always be with them, even though they will not see him. **Jesus** wants nothing of this world to come between you and him. Satan will use the riches of this world to keep you from listening to your **Lord**. If you are not struggling financially; then be very careful to use the excess for the glory of **God**. And if you are considered poor, and are not serving **Jesus** daily; then guess what? You really are poor! But if you are thankful for your grace from **God**, and are working for the **Lord daily**, then you are one of the richest of heaven!

Mankind has it in their heads that **Jesus** rewards the obedient with things of this world; but the things of this world are only temporary. Most of the rewards that **Jesus** gives you are eternal!

The rewards that **Jesus** has for you may not be seen in this life. Some of the rewards can be seen immediately, such as healing of the body, knowledge, wisdom, etc....

But the big rewards will be waiting for you in your permanent home in heaven, if you are going there! If you are not a born again Christian, then you will not have any need for rewards where you are going!

Do not make fun of the poor, but help them anyway you can. And always be thankful for your blessings.

Pray and ask **Jesus** every day what you can do for him. Because if you have received him as your **Lord and Savior**; then he have already taken care of you……..eternity! Thank you Jesus! Thank you God and thank you Holy Ghost!

WHO TOUCHED ME?

(Luke 8:43 thru 48)

43) And a woman having an issue of blood twelve years, which had spent all her living upon physicians, neither could be healed of any,

44) Came behind **him**, *and touched the border of* **his** *garment: and immediately her issue of blood stanched.*

45) And **Jesus** *said* **who touched me?** *When all denied, Peter and they that were with him said, Master, the multitude throng thee and press thee, and sayest thou, who touched me?*

46) And **Jesus** *said someone hath touched* **me**.*: for* **I** *perceive that virtue is gone out of* **me**.

47)And when the woman saw that she was not hid, she came trembling, and falling down before **him**, *and she declared unto* **him** *before all the people for what cause she had touched* **him**, *and how she was healed immediately.*

48) And **he** *said unto her, Daughter, be of good comfort: thy faith hath made thee whole; go in peace.*

This instance is so awesome! Here is **Jesus** walking to the next city to preach; and there is a large crowd of people around **him**. At this particular moment, **he** is not healing anyone. But **Jesus** is so powerful that **he** heals without even focusing. The woman was completely healed from the blood issue that she and the physicians had been fighting for twelve years.

But if it had not been for the woman's faith, she would not have been cured that day. Not because **Jesus** couldn't; but because **he** wouldn't!

After she confessed to touching **Jesus** and why, **Jesus** told her to go in peace; that her faith had made her whole.

This woman knew and believed in **Jesus**. She didn't even try to touch **him**; only his garment. She knew that his power would be sufficient for her needs.

And the power **Jesus** had back then; **he** still has today! **His** power was sufficient back then, and is still sufficient for our needs today. But we also must believe that this is true. That way our belief in **Christ Jesus** will heal us too!

Do you believe in **Jesus**? Do you know him personally? **He** sure knows you!

WHO WROTE THE BIBLE?

I have heard the comment made many times that the Bible was written by man's hands. Therefore it must be fake. But I say this to those who might believe that comment. Yes man wrote the Bible; but it was under **God's** direction, and with **God's words!**

(Jeremiah 36:1 thru 3)

1) *And it came to pass in the fourth year of Je-hoi`a-kim the son of Jo-si`-ah king of Judah, that this word came unto Jer-e-mi`-ah from* **the Lord**, *saying,*

2) *Take thee a roll of a book, and write therein all the words that* **I** *have spoken unto thee against Israel, and against Judah, and against all the nations, from the day* **I** *spake unto thee, from the days of Jo-si`-ah, even into this day.*

3) *It may be that the house of Judah will hear all the evil which I purpose to do unto them; that they may return every man from his evil way; that I may forgive their iniquity and their sin.*

There is one example of when **God** told one of his prophets, to record what **God** had told Jeremiah what to say.

Another verse to behold is in the book of Revelation.

(Revelation 22:7)

Behold, I come quickly; blessed is he that keepeth the sayings of the prophecy of this book.

Do not let any-ones unbelief in the word of **God**, to cause any doubt in your hearts, or minds. Just stand strong on his word!

WHY AM I HATED BY SO MANY PEOPLE?

(John 17:14)

I have given them thy word; and the world hath hated them, because they are not of the world, even as I am not of the world.

If you are truly born again then you are not of this world anymore. You no longer wish to please mankind, but would rather please your Savior. Because you no longer wish to participate in the evil things that most of the people are doing; you are no longer accepted by them. Most will even hate you!

(John 17:15)

I pray not that thou shouldest take them out of the world, but that thou shouldest keep them from the evil.

Jesus is praying to God for his children to be protected from the evil of Satan, but that they should remain in the world, so they can tell others about Jesus. Not being of the world, but in the world!

Non-believers hate Christians because they first hated Christ! If you are being talked about and ridiculed because of Jesus, then rejoice and be of good cheer, for great is your reward in heaven!

WHY AM I WORKING HERE?

Dear **Lord**, why am I surrounded by so many immoral people at work? Has no one at work heard about you? Why am I working with all these sinners?

Boy was I reminded why it is that I am working here when **Jesus** answered my question. He reminded me that **he** is the reason that I am surrounded by so many immoral people. He said a long time ago to the scribes and Pharisees, and it goes for me and you also!

(Luke 5:31 and 32)

And **Jesus** *answering said unto them,* **they that are whole need not a physician; but they that are sick. I came not to call the righteous, but sinners to repentance.**

He told me as one of his followers, that I am in that location **for him**! **Not me!** He said that my salvation is sealed. But others are not so fortunate. He said that he sent his brothers (us) to tell them how to find **him!**

WHY DID JESUS COME TO EARTH?

(John 3:17 thru 21)

17) For God sent <u>*not*</u> *his Son into the world to condemn the world; but that the world through him might be saved.*

18) He that believeth on **him** *is not condemned: but he that believeth not is condemned already, because he hath not believed in the name of the* **only begotten son of God**.

19) And this is the condemnation, that light is come into the world, and men loved darkness rather than light, because there deeds were evil.

20) For every one that doeth evil hateth the light, neither come to the light, lest his deeds should be reproved.

21) But he that doeth truth cometh to the light, that his deeds may be made manifest, that they are wrought in **God**.

Jesus loves you so much! He wants you to have the best things that **God** has to offer you, not what man has for you. He came here to save as many of his brothers and sisters as will believe. Unfortunately there will be a lot of God's creations that will be condemned, and will find there selves in Hell one day! The way to heaven is so simple, thanks to **Jesus**. He did most of the work! But if you do not believe in him and do not accept him for the light and truth that he is; then you do not have a future that I want to talk about. I will cry for you now, because there will be <u>no</u> <u>tears</u> where I am going!

Are you condemned already? Or are you saved?

WHY GOD; WHY DO WE DIE?

(Genesis 2:16 & 17)

16) *And the Lord God commanded the man, saying, of every tree of the garden thou mayest freely eat!*

17) But of the tree of the knowledge of good and evil, thou shalt not eat of it: **for in the day that thou eatest thereof thou shalt surely die.**

(Genesis 3:4-7)

4) And the serpent said unto the woman, ye shall not surely die:

5) For God doth know that in the day ye eat thereof, then your eyes shall be opened, and ye shall be as Gods, knowing good and evil.

6) And when the woman saw that the tree was good for food, and that it was pleasant to the eyes, and a tree to be desired to make one wise, she took of the fruit thereof, and did eat, and gave also unto her husband with her; and he did eat.

7) And the eyes of them both were opened, and they knew that they were naked; and they sewed fig leaves together, and made themselves aprons.

Was God angry? This is what he told Adam and Eve

(Genesis 3:19)

19) In the sweat of thy face shalt thou eat bread, till thou return unto the ground: for out of it wast thou taken: **for dust thou art, and unto dust shalt thou return.**

Now that we know why we have to die, our next question should be, is this world all that there is? Do we just cease to exist? Who will save us from death?

(John 3:16)

16) For **GOD** *so loved the world, that he gave his only begotten son, that whosoever believeth in him should not perish, but have ever-lasting life.*

Now because of **Jesus, Gods only son, who died on the cross to save believers from their sin**; we have another life after this one! Only the next life will never end!

My family lost a good friend this week in a car accident. And the reason it is so hard for me to understand why **God** took her; is that she had a husband who loved her very much. Two young beautiful girls that are so much like her it's almost spooky. And she had a step son to boost her life even more! She was not old, or sick or troubled mentally (depressed). She seemed to me to have life under control; and now she is gone home.

But for me personally she is not gone forever from me. She was a born again Christian (Believer in Christ), and so am I. So one day when **God** calls me home; I will be with my sister again! Is she gone forever from your life; or will you see her again also?

WILL WE MARRY IN HEAVEN?

(Luke 20:34-35)

And Jesus answering said unto them, The children of this world marry; and are given in marriage:

But they which shall be accounted worthy to obtain that world, and the resurrection from the dead, neither marry or are given in marriage.

When Jesus died on the cross to forgive us of our sins; God gave him full authority over our salvation! You simply cannot be saved by anyone or anything other than Jesus! He is the only one who can forgive us of our sins, and when God raised Jesus up from the grave; it is Jesus that will say who goes with him into God's kingdom. No one else!

We will not marry because those who believe in the truth will be united with our savior forever!

WIN-WIN SITUATION

In the business world there is a brilliant rule that states: Always create a win-win situation. It simply means that when you make any decision, make it one that benefits the company and the customer. It makes perfect sense! If both parties benefit, then you have a great chance of the two parties doing business again.

Relationships of every kind prosper from the same principle. Marriage, Kin, Friendship, Neighbors etc…

Where did this incredible idea come from? Who could be so smart to think of this principle?

God is the one who came up with this principle, and all good principles. He created an entire universe with this idea.

Everything he made works in perfect harmony together. But the evil one (Satan) came into the picture and offered another idea. Do evil to others before they do evil unto you.

So now you have a choice!

(Luke 6:31)

And as ye would that men should do to you, do ye also to them likewise. Do unto others as you would have done unto you

If you will use this principle in your life at all times, and in every situation; then your rewards are going to be great! But if you follow the advice of Satan; then you are going to deal with pain and sorrow! Make the right choice!

WISDOM AND KNOWLEDGE

Wisdom: Good practical judgment; common sense.

Know-ledge: Information or understanding acquired through experience; practical ability; or skill.

(1 Corinthians 12:4-8, 12-13)

4) Now there are diversities of gifts, but the same spirit.

5) And there are differences of administrations, but the same Lord.

6) And there are diversities of operations, but it is the same God which worketh all in all.

7) But the manifestation of the Spirit is given to every man to profit withal.

8) For to one is given by the Spirit the word of wisdom; to another the word of knowledge by the same Spirit;

12) For as the body is one, and hath many members, and all the members of that one body, being many, are one body: so also is Christ.

13) For by one Spirit are we all baptized into one body, whether we be Jews or Gentiles, whether we be bond or free; and have been all made to drink into one Spirit.

As you can see, all of us have been blessed with some kind of gift or gifts by the same Holy Spirit. It is our responsibility to talk to God and find out what our gift(s) are. Then after we know, then we need to use them for Gods will. Remember that Faith without works is dead! We should be thrilled to do our part for our Lord.

We have a great opportunity in our area. There is a lot of new neighbor's right outside our church doors. We have new people in our membership who are eager to do Gods work. We have a lot of older members who have a lot of knowledge. And best of all we have an all-mighty God to help us every step of the way! So let's get going and tell everyone about the greatest gift of all: God's only son Jesus Christ! WOW! WHAT A SAVIOUR!

YE ARE MY FRIENDS

(John 15: 14 thru 17)

14) Ye are my friends, if ye do whatsoever I command you.

15) Henceforth I call you not servants; for the servant knoweth not what his lord doeth: but I have called you friends; for all things that I have heard of my Father I have made known unto you.

16) Ye have not chosen me, but I have chosen you, and ordained you, that ye should go and bring forth fruit, and that your fruit should remain: and whatsoever ye shall ask of the Father in my name, he may give it to you.

17) These things I command you, that ye love one another.

When I read these verses, the Lord touched my heart. Up until this time in my spiritual life I had called myself a servant of Christ. But he let me know that it is now time to change my thinking, and feelings. Even though I am still a sinner in my flesh, he let me know that because I know that he is working in my life; and I know what his intentions are; and I am willing to do what he says, that I am his friend!

Again I stand in amazement that the only God of Heaven; the maker of all things known to man; that he would not only allow me to be one of his son's friends; but commands it!

And that Jesus himself wants me for a friend. Thank you Jesus for having me as a friend! I pray that I will be a true and trustworthy one for ever more!

ABOUT THE AUTHOR

I am an extremely thankful born again Christian just to be a part of this book. I am relying on Gods grace everyday, just like millions of other Christians do. I am a forty nine year old, married man with four children, and we have four grandchildren. I work at a soft drink company, and now find that I have been blessed to write a book for God! I never asked God for this book, he chose me! God has truly blessed me in so many ways; especially allowing me to know and walk with his son Jesus!

You will find the Holy Bible in most homes, but very few people take the time to read the incredible truths that are inside. My prayer is that this book will tempt you to read, and study the word of God. The Holy Bible is God's word to mankind; and is full of miraculous true stories that happened in the past; and are still happening today! God is still in charge!

I pray God blesses you and your family with this book.

James Andrew Feather 1st.